Practical social wor

**Published in conjunction with
the British Association of Social Workers**

 BASW
THE BRITISH ASSOCIATION OF SOCIAL WORKERS

Founding editor: Jo Campling

Social Work is a multi-skilled profession, centred on people. Social workers need skills in problem-solving, communication, critical reflection and working with others to be effective in practice.

The British Association of Social Workers (www.basw.co.uk) has always been conscious of its role in setting guidelines for practice and in seeking to raise professional standards. The concept of the Practical Social Work series was developed to fulfil a genuine professional need for a carefully planned, coherent, series of texts that would contribute to practitioners' skills, development and professionalism.

Newly relaunched to meet the ever-changing needs of the social work profession, the series has been reviewed and revised with the help of the BASW Editorial Advisory Board:

Peter Beresford
Jim Campbell
Monica Dowling
Brian Littlechild
Mark Lymbery
Fraser Mitchell
Steve Moore

Under their guidance each book marries practice issues with theory and research in a compact and applied format: perfect for students, practitioners and educators.

A comprehensive list of titles available in the series can be found online at: www.palgrave.com/socialwork/basw

---

Series standing order **ISBN 0–333–80313–2**

You can receive future titles in this series as they are published by placing a standing order. Please contact your bookseller or, in the case of difficulty, contact us at the address below with your name and address, the title of the series and the ISBN quoted above.

Customer Services Department, Macmillan Distribution Ltd, Houndmills, Basingstoke, Hampshire RG21 6XS, England

Practical social work series

New titles

Sarah Banks *Ethics and Values in Social Work* **(4th edition)**

Veronica Coulshed and Joan Orme *Social Work Practice* **(5th edition)**

Veronica Coulshed, Audrey Mullender and Margaret McClade *Management in Social Work* **(4th edition) Coming soon!**

Celia Doyle *Working with Abused Children* **(4th edition)**

Gordon Jack and Helen Donnellan *Social Work with Children* **Coming soon!**

Paula Nicolson and Rowan Bayne *Psychology for Social Work Theory and Practice* **(4th edition) Coming soon!**

Michael Oliver, Bob Sapey and Pamela Thomas *Social Work with Disabled People* **(4th edition)**

Mo Ray and Judith Philips *Social Work with Older People* **(5th edition)**

Steven Shardlow and Mark Doel *Practice Learning and Teaching* **(2nd edition) Coming soon!**

Neil Thompson *Anti-Discriminatory Practice* **(5th edition)**

For further companion resources visit www.palgrave.com/socialwork/basw

Mo Ray
and
Judith Phillips

Social Work with Older People

Fifth Edition

First edition (entitled *Social Work with Old People*) 1983
Reprints unknown
Second edition (entitled *Social Work with Old People*) 1990
Reprinted twice
Third edition 1996
Reprinted four times
Fourth edition 2006
Reprinted five times
Fifth edition 2012

Published by
PALGRAVE MACMILLAN

Palgrave Macmillan in the UK is an imprint of Macmillan Publishers
Limited, registered in England, company number 785998, of Houndmills,
Basingstoke, Hampshire RG21 6XS.

Palgrave Macmillan in the US is a division of St Martin's Press LLC,
175 Fifth Avenue, New York, NY 10010.

Palgrave Macmillan is the global academic imprint of the above companies
and has companies and representatives throughout the world.

Palgrave® and Macmillan® are registered trademarks in the United States,
the United Kingdom, Europe and other countries

ISBN-13: 978–0–230–30047–7

This book is printed on paper suitable for recycling and made from fully
managed and sustained forest sources. Logging, pulping and manufacturing
processes are expected to conform to the environmental regulations of
the country of origin.

A catalogue record for this book is available from the British Library.

A catalog record for this book is available from the Library of Congress.

10   9   8   7   6   5   4   3   2   1
21   20   19   18   17   16   15   14   13   12

Printed in China

Mo Ray: to Brian Joyce, with love and thanks

Judith Phillips: to Peter

Brief Contents

Contents

List of tables, figures and boxes

Tables

Figures

Boxes

Acknowledgements

We acknowledge those who taught us and inspired us to pursue a career in social work and also the practitioners, older men and women and students we have subsequently worked with. Mo Ray wishes to thank colleagues Mim Bernard, Judith Phillips and Pat Chambers. Judith Phillips would like to thank Teresa Smith who continues to inspire her and the Fellows of New College, Oxford who supported her study leave. We would also like to thank: Mary Pat Sullivan, Alisoun Milne, Sally Richards, Denise Tanner, Christian Beech and Liz Lloyd; Mary Gilhooly and Christina Victor at Brunel University, and Kate Llewellyn at Palgrave.

List of abbreviations

BSP	Basic State Pension
CQC	Care Quality Commission (formerly CSCI)
CSCI	Commission for Social Care Inspection (now CQC)
DoH	Department of Health
ECSH	Extra Care Sheltered Housing
FACS	Fair Access to Care Services
HMSO	Her Majesty's Stationery Office
ONS	Office of National Statistics
RAS	Resource Allocation System
RNIB	Royal National Institute for Blind People
RNID	Royal National Institute for Deaf People (now called Action on Hearing Loss)
SCIE	Social Care Institute for Excellence
SSI	Social Services Inspectorate
WHO	World Health Organisation

Key legislation

Adult Support and Protection (Scotland) Act (2007)
Beveridge Report (1942)
Care Standards Act (2000)
Carers and Disabled Children Act (2000)
Carers (Equal Opportunites) Act (2005)
Children Act (1990)
Chronically Sick and Disabled Persons Act (1970)
Community Care (Direct Payments) Act 1995
Criminal Justice Act (2003)
Data Protection Act (1998)
Disability Discrimination Act (1995)
Disability Discrimination Act (2005)
Domestic Violence, Crime and Victims Act (2004)
Health Act (1999)
Health Services and Public Health Act (1968)
Health and Social Care Act (2001)
Health and Social Care Act (2008)
Human Rights Act (1988)
Mental Capacity Act (2005)
Mental Health Act (1959)
Mental Health Act (1983)
Mental Health Act (2007)
National Assistance Act (1948)
National Health Service Act (2006)
National Health Service and Community Care Act (1990)
Public Interest Disclosure Act (1998)
Race Relations (Amendment) Act (2000)
Safeguarding Vulnerable Groups Act (2006)

Introduction

This book aims to inspire and inform social workers and social work students who want to know more about working with older people and their families. It will also be helpful for professionals who work with social workers and want to understand more about their special contribution. It is written by people with long experience in the field: in practice, as social workers, undertaking research in this field and teaching gerontology and social work. It is an introductory text offering a good grounding in some of the complex issues surrounding social work with older people; the assumption is that enthusiasts will move on to read more of what is now a substantial literature about older people, if not about social work specifically. It is quite impossible for one volume to cover the whole field thoroughly, but a book like this can whet the appetite and can point in the direction of further reading. Most of the relevant literature is not written specifically for social workers, so this book is a rich source of references to a very wide range of material.

Social work with older people has many dimensions and raises many dilemmas. At a time of great change in the landscape of social work, this book attempts to addresses a range of relevant topics and map out some of the complexities of practice with older people. We have aimed to target a beginning practitioner who has a special interest in older people. Social work with older people is complex and the book attempts to examine the values, skills and knowledge required to work with older people, as well as embracing a wider perspective than the 'personalisation agenda'. In this way it provides a specific contribution to the literature.

Social workers who choose this field cannot be shrinking violets. Older people are not well served by social workers who do not question attitudes, resources and priorities. Ageism is rife and one manifestation is the widespread assumption that older people have simple needs, such as for food, warmth, cleanliness and safety, whereas the reality is that what they need is effective and skilful practice. Simply filling in forms and brokering care are rarely an adequate response. The much overworked, and insufficiently practised, concept of community care can too easily become community neglect, at least of the unique individuality of each older person and their particular circumstances.

Current policy, in the English context, is driving the agenda towards individual budgets and direct payments. This represents a significant change in the way personal social services are arranged and delivered, and the importance of people who use services being able to exercise choice and control over how their support needs are met and by whom is identified as a fundamental principle. Nevertheless, it is important to adopt an open and questioning approach to this personalisation in respect of older people in order that we can uncover potential obstacles, challenges or ethical dilemmas. The role for social work in the context of personalisation remains unclear (Lymbery and Postle, 2010), with a notable absence of recognition of the role that professional social work should and can yet play in adult personal social services. This book attempts to do just that, as well as recognising that the policy context in the devolved nations is increasingly divergent from that in England. These differences are highlighted in some areas of the book, but it is beyond its remit to explore their implications in all areas of social work practice with older people. In broad terms, the content of the book remain relevant to all practitioners.

Social workers also need to be confident that they have something special to offer. Government policy is rightly pushing towards teamwork and sharing skills, but this cannot be achieved to best effect unless everyone in the team knows what particular contribution they can make. While there are large areas of overlap, there are also very specific areas of knowledge and skill. We provide a clear picture of what we believe these to be. We also give very clear messages about a value base that emphasises participation, sharing information, being open about what we are doing and avoiding oppressive practice.

This is the fifth edition of this book. The first was published in 1983 in a very different world. The baby boomers of the turn of the century were ageing and few social workers were interested in their care. The field of gerontology was emerging and the pluralist economy of care was unknown. Twenty years later, the shape of the ageing population is very different and we have experienced a great shift in the way services are delivered. We are also perhaps wiser, both about social work with older people and about older people generally; there is now a very substantial body of research and writing in this area. We can, for example, talk about the evidence base for some of our work, although a great deal more research is still needed.

At the time of writing, the landscape of social work itself is also undergoing significant change. Following the review of the role and purpose of social work, implementation of the 15 recommendations made in the Department of Health 2009 report has been ongoing in England (Department of Health, 2009c). The recommendations include the development of a professional standards framework with clearly defined expectations of social workers at various stages of their career, including newly qualified social workers. For newly qualified workers, an assessed and supported year in practice (ASYE) is in development to ensure that they receive consistent support and that their practice is consistent with the professional standards expected of a newly qualified practitioner. It is anticipated that the ASYE will have to be completed successfully in order to continue to practice as a social worker.

The Reform Board recommendations include a move away from competence-based training to a Professional Capabilities Framework (Department of Health/ADASS, 2010), which will define how a social worker's knowledge, skills and capacity should develop over the course of their career. Critics of a competence-based approach to training in social work have argued that 'a functional analysis of concrete, observable tasks and behaviors is simply inappropriate for complex "professional activities" ', that it ignores the potential for professional judgement, takes no account of group processes and has no regard for the influence of social context or setting (Cooper, 2008: 227). A capabilities approach to social work training and ongoing professional development moves away from demonstrating 'competence' to developing practitioners who can exercise sound professional judgement and the 'ability to demonstrate "expertise in action" ' (Cooper, 2008: 231). The nine core capabilities proposed by the Reform Board are of relevance to all social workers regardless of their area of practice or their level of experience:

- *Professionalism* – identify and behave as a professional social worker, committed to professional development.
- *Values and ethics* – apply social work ethical principles and values to guide professional practice.
- *Diversity* – recognise diversity and apply anti-discriminatory and anti-oppressive principles in practice.

- *Rights, justice and economic wellbeing* – advance human rights and promote social justice and economic wellbeing.
- *Knowledge* – apply knowledge of social sciences, law and social work practice theory.
- *Critical reflection and analysis* – apply critical reflection and analysis to inform and provide a rationale for professional decision making.
- *Intervention and skills* – use judgement and authority to intervene with individuals, families and communities to promote independence, provide support and prevent harm, neglect and abuse.
- *Contexts and organisations* – engage with, inform and adapt to changing contexts that shape practice. Operate effectively in the own organisational frameworks and contribute to the development of services and organisations.
- *Professional leadership* – take responsibility for the professional learning and development of others through supervision, mentoring, assessing, research, leadership, teaching and management (Department for Education, 2010).

This book will be useful in encouraging readers to relate the capabilities framework to effective, professional practice with older people.

The book is divided into two parts. Part I addresses the context of social work with older people and draws heavily on gerontological literature; Part II addresses practice issues. Throughout, we attempt to integrate both social work and gerontological literatures and provide a critical perspective that challenges traditional assumptions about older people.

Chapter 1 maps out the crucial issues facing older people in our society today: how older people are defined, the situations in which they live, and the role they play in society. These aspects highlight the diversity of older people and the context of ageing in Britain.

Chapter 2 focuses on a case for social work, and asks who social work is for and under what circumstances it operates. Not all older people, even those in later life and in difficult circumstances, will come the way of social workers. The reasons for intervention are often the many and complex problems that older people face. The chapter concludes by reviewing some of the frameworks that guide intervention: theory, reflexivity, evidence- or knowledge-based research, policy and legislation.

Policy and its organisational context are discussed further in

Chapter 3, which briefly looks at the historical development of services for older people and the changing nature of policy and legislation in the past 20 years focusing primarily on England. Despite the expansion of legislation and guidance and the introduction of the personalisation agenda, social workers face continued organisational constraints and pressures. This chapter addresses the difficulties of working in different social work contexts.

Chapter 4 explores the issue of safeguarding in social work with older people.

The role, tasks and skills necessary in social work are discussed in Part II. We look at the role of assessment, support planning and intervention and the necessity of reviewing support plans and interventions. By reading this book we hope that social workers will become critical practitioners able to intervene more effectively in anti-oppressive, participatory and empowering ways.

Most people learn through stories and this book provides several. They come from real practice and are presented to enable the reader to think through the issues. As in all fields, and perhaps especially so for a low-status group of service users, we need social workers who can reflect on their practice.

Throughout the book we draw on different approaches to illustrate various points and to encourage the active participation of readers. It is hoped that they will encourage readers to reflect on the issues raised and to consider them with respect to their own practice. The longer case studies can be a useful tool for discussion and debate in a learning environment.

Each chapter starts by summarising the key points of the chapter in order to signpost the reader to the different topics and debates they will read about. Throughout the book, the reader can find out more about key research on older people in the 'Messages from Research' boxes in each chapter. The 'Point for reflection' boxes invite the reader to reflect on the material presented in the book or to relate the material to their own practical experience.

There are a number of terms that the reader will find repeated throughout the book, reflecting the critical perspectives from which we write. For example, we place the emphasis on 'ageing' rather than 'old age'. This latter term, as we discuss in Chapter 1, is socially constructed and we prefer to take a longer life course approach. Some may argue that ageing begins as soon as we are born! We also prefer to use the term 'older people' rather than 'the elderly', which stigmatises and homogenises the 50 years – or more – of life that can be experienced under this term. A great deal has been written in the literature about the 'third' and 'fourth' ages or the 'young' old (up to 75 years of age) and the 'old' old. We move away from these false distinctions as ageing becomes an experience that we all share. Taking older people as people first and also as citizens, however complex their health needs may be, reflects the value position that we adopt in this book. It is a position that has underpinned our professional work as practitioners, lecturers and researchers in the field of ageing.

We want to introduce readers to the concept of gerontological social work as a significant area of work with an increasing knowledge base. This is a common term used in the United States to distinguish this as an area of practice with a history and an established evidence base. It has applicability not only in the UK but worldwide, as other societies grapple with similar issues surrounding an ageing population, and it is our hope that this book will mark the beginning of a trend towards gerontological social work.

This book refers to English legislation and UK government policies and documents alone. Most of these apply to England, Wales and Northern Ireland, but policy in the devolved nations is becoming increasingly divergent, with a plethora of legislation and documentation, so it should not be assumed that policy in adult social care is developing in precisely the same way. However, all the nations have policies on social care, closer cooperation between health and social work, attending to the needs of carers, user consultation and greater monitoring of standards, so readers in Scotland, Northern Ireland and Wales will still find this book entirely relevant.

The book can be read from beginning to end, but it can also be dipped into. It provides further references to texts covering issues in greater depth and several websites, which will help readers keep up to date with the issues. At the end of each chapter is a section called 'Putting it into practice', setting out two or three exercises that may be helpful in reflecting on the chapter.

As you work through the book, you will develop your knowledge, understanding and skills in relation to social work with older people. Alongside this, you will develop a critical and reflexive perspective, your analytical skills and your ability to use research in practice.

PART I

The Social Work Context

CHAPTER 1

Critical themes and issues in ageing

CHAPTER OVERVIEW

- Social workers work with older people who are likely to have complex and high support needs – but older people are far from a homogenous group.
- Those in the older population are characterised by diversity and difference in terms of their structural location (for example birth cohort, gender, ethnicity, culture) as well as in their individual biographies.
- There remain significant differences in life expectancy between men and women.
- While the age structure of black and minority ethnic groups is still rather younger than that of the white majority population, this is slowly changing.
- There are considerable differences in health experiences among older people. While significant numbers of older people report living with a long-term condition – or conditions – most older people also describe their health as good.
- It is estimated that 1.5 million older people are occupied with informal care and a significant number of those people care for someone with whom they live.
- The diversity of ageing experience sets the scene for diverse social work practice that must be underpinned by an open-minded approach and a commitment to challenge stereotyped assumptions about ageing and age-based discrimination.

Introduction

In this chapter we set the scene for the context of social work with older people by outlining the key themes and issues in ageing. We deliberately take a critical gerontological approach from the outset.

This is in preference to presenting basic facts and figures and outlining the problems that older people face. Although social workers need to know the details and consequences of population ageing, they also need to reframe some perspectives through which older people have been stereotyped, for example as burdens on society by virtue of their numbers and being dependent on family members. By the nature of their role and tasks social workers work with older people with the most complex needs, but they need to take a wider perspective in order to understand the diversity of ageing and to view experiences in later life in a positive light, rather than treating ageing necessarily as a negative experience. Even when people face crises, the strengths they have developed and demonstrated throughout their life course need to be acknowledged and worked with by social work practitioners. It is imperative that social workers understand and take a critical approach in their practice if they are to work effectively with older people in an anti-discriminatory way.

It is important, first, to look at the people we are talking about and the situations faced by an ageing population. After defining and critically evaluating the concepts of 'ageing' and 'old age', we look at the diversity of the older population in terms of structural factors such as gender, ethnicity and class. We then move on to look at variations in how people experience ageing and later life based on differences in location, housing and living arrangements and health. All these factors, along with more individual factors such as relationships and social support, will have an impact on their quality of life. The challenge for social workers is to operate within this diverse context in a positive way, challenging the myths that ageing is inevitably a period of decline and that older people with complex needs can no longer experience a good life.

Defining ageing: What is 'old'?

There have been shifting definitions of 'old' throughout history. Whereas 200 years ago someone aged 40 might have seemed 'old', today they would be considered 'young' or in the prime of their life. Legal institutions and bureaucracies tend to define 'old' by chronological age, often as a means of demonstrating eligibility for particular services, for example age-related eligibility for free bus passes or pensions. Definitions and expressions of age also differ across cultures. For instance, in Bosnia old age is not linked to chronological age or external appearance but a 'loss of power' (Vincent, 2003: 15), referring to both physical and social strength.

Longevity has been the success story of modern society, with more of the population living longer into old age. General improvements in public health, housing, food supplies and working conditions have greatly improved our standard of living. This has meant that more people have survived beyond infancy and lived into adulthood, stretching the definition of 'old'. A boy born in 1901 could expect to live to 45 and a girl to 49; today these figures are 77.2 and 81.5 years respectively (ONS, 2009). There are almost half a million people in Britain aged 90 or over and the numbers of centenarians in the UK has more than quadrupled, from 2600 in 1981 to 11,600 in 2010 (ONS, 2010b). It is the rapid increase in the proportion of the 85-plus age group in comparison to older people in general that is significant for the planning of social and health care services, as disability tends to increase with later life. Whether as a society we will be able to sustain such increases in longevity is a moot point, however, as obesity in childhood, inadequate diet and lack of exercise with increases in alcohol consumption all threaten this trend.

Our subjective assessment of age is, however, governed by the ways in which ageing may be defined or constructed. For example, we may be informed by chronologically based definitions of age such as formal retirement ages, eligibility for subsidised public transport and winter fuel allowances, or age-based access to health care and health screening. Perceptions of old age may focus on notions of dependency and vulnerability; in our own profession, we have a tendency to focus on dysfunction in older age as a means of determining eligibility for services, which is too often at the expense of recognising the strengths and resources on which older people are able to draw in later life. While this book will inevitably focus on the kind of needs that social work practitioners working with older people are likely to encounter in their practice, we must not forget that any discussion about ageing should be underpinned by an understanding of its diversity and a recognition that older people are not a homogenous group. On the contrary, while research may report trends or patterns in the experience of ageing, it remains the case that ageing should be seen as an experience unique to the individual and characterised by heterogeneity.

As we discuss later in this chapter, social resources through family and friends are an important factor in later life.

Nevertheless, family life has changed with rising divorce rates, reconstituted families, later marriages and age-gapped families, along with geographical distance between generations. This also means that different generations and cohorts will experience family life very differently. Unlike any previous generation, a larger percentage of older people over the age of 60 will be entering old age as divorced, will have had experience of second or multiple marriages and partnerships and may have a large network of step-children and grandchildren. With remarriage and divorce, older people may experience a transition to other intimate partnerships.

Increasingly, healthy older people enjoy activities that have traditionally been associated with 'youth' and continue to enjoy hobbies in which they have participated throughout their life course as well as starting new interests. These experiences are no longer exceptional.

Older people contribute significantly in all areas of social life, for example through ongoing provision of support (practical, emotional, financial) to adult offspring or to grandchildren and other family members needing care. They also participate in a range of citizenship roles (for example the magistracy, parish councils, prison monitoring boards; all of which, however, still have age cut-off points) and through the provision of human resources, skill and expertise in the voluntary sector.

At the other extreme, there are older people who have experienced poverty for much or all of their lives. Social exclusion from, for example, good-quality housing, regular paid work, access to health care and living in vibrant and well-resourced communities is often an associated consequence of living in poverty. In older age, people may experience a continuity of poverty, which could be worsened by ageing (for example as a result of widowhood or the experience of illness). Older people may have managed during their lives but may experience poverty in retirement because they do not have access to adequate pensions. Around 17 per cent of people receiving state pensions are defined as living in poverty, with single, retired females being most at risk of poverty or living on a severely reduced income (www.poverty.org.uk). This problem is exacerbated by the consistently low take-up of benefit entitlements (such as pension credit, council tax relief and housing benefit). Approximately one third of all pensioner households entitled to pension credit are not claiming it (that is, 1.3 million households) and two-fifths of all pensioner households entitled to council tax benefit are not claiming that (that is, 1.7 million households) (www.poverty.org.uk).

Older women: The 'feminisation of ageing'

The world of 'old age' is traditionally a world of women. Differences in the proportions of men and women in old age arise from women's higher life expectancy. At all ages, the older population is disproportionately female. However, the ratio of women to men among people aged 65 and over is falling. In 1983 there were 155 women aged 65 and over for every 100 men of the same age. Currently, there are 130 women for every 100 men aged 65 and over. By 2033 this figure is expected to be 117 women for every 100 men (ONS, 2010).

The reasons for the difference in longevity remain unclear, but include the greater likelihood of men experiencing life-threatening illness resulting in death compared to women, who are more likely to experience long-term, chronic and disabling conditions. Increased longevity for women, together with features common to women's lives, results in particular consequences for older women. For example, traditionally women have tended to marry or partner with men older than themselves and this means they are more likely to care for their husbands, as well as to be widows. In 2006, for example, 62 per cent of men aged 75 and over were married compared to 28 per cent of women; 27 per cent of men aged 75 and over were widowed compared to 60 per cent of women (ONS, 2007). Chambers (2005) has commented that widowhood is a normative expectation for heterosexual women as they move into older age. It also follows that women experience widowhood for longer than their male counterparts are widowers. Without the possibility of getting care from their spouse, widows who become disabled and ill are more likely than men to enter residential care (ONS, 2010). The same is true for women who have never married. So 6 per cent of older women aged 65 and over live in residential care, compared to 3 per cent of men in the same age group. The figure rises to 23 per cent of women aged 85 and over, compared to 12 per cent of men in the same age group (ONS, 2010).

Women are also more likely to have had sparse or interrupted work records. Apart from during the war, in the 1930s, 1940s and 1950s married women were discouraged from working. Significant disruption to working life to provide care for children and other family care giving remains a common experience for women. Given the potential for interruptions to work, and a reliance at least some of the time on part-time work, women are much less likely to have contributed to their own pensions, or their pension contributions are inadequate (ONS, 2010). There is greater reliance on state pension provision among older women, and older women living alone are likely to be the most deprived. A larger proportion of women than of men receive less than the full basic state pension (BSP). In 2008, 34 per cent of female pensioners (2.3 million women) received 60 per cent of full BSP or less, compared with 2 per cent of male pensioners (under 0.1 million) (ONS, 2010).

Starting in 2010, Parliament has enacted a number of pension reforms, designed to transform the nature of state pension provision so that, for example, 95 per cent of both men and women pensioners should be on full BSP by 2050. Acquiring a pension through a husband's earnings is becoming increasingly risky because of the propensity for divorce and the evidence base highlighting the likelihood of greater financial vulnerability for women living alone in older age (ONS, 2010; Burholt and Windle, 2006). The National Pensioners Convention has argued for a gender-oriented pensions policy that addresses the inequalities in income caused by employment patterns and caring commitments, as well as providing survivor benefits in recognition of the gendered mortality differential and likelihood of being a widow (www.pcs.org.uk, 2008).

Although the social networks of older women are more extensive than men's, the majority of older women whom social workers meet live alone. For women increasing age is closely associated with living alone: over 60 per cent of women aged 75 and over live alone (ONS, 2010). Research has suggested a relationship between loneliness and sociodemographic factors, including being female, being widowed and living alone (Victor et al., 2005).

Until the 1980s women were invisible in social policy. However, this situation has changed and care services are increasingly gender sensitive. In residential care, for example, women over the age of 85 are over-represented, along with those older people who have previously lived alone. Increasingly, issues over the funding of long-term care, the closure of care homes and the movement of older people between care homes, when they can no longer afford to pay or where homes have closed, have had a disproportionately negative impact on women.

There is circularity in the feminisation of the caring relationship. Many of those living in care homes are cared for by women who may be engaged in informal care (for relatives) as well as in a formal (paid) capacity (Cameron and Phillips, 2003). Work routines in care homes may facilitate part-time employment to enable women to manage other caring responsibilities, and the pay and conditions are often at the national minimum. The scene is set for future generations of women engaged in this type of work to experience the poverty of their older counterparts.

Cuts in community services, particularly in relation to transport, are also likely to affect women significantly. Women are more likely to rely on public transport than men and generally have less opportunity to drive cars than men, thus, in later life, accessibility becomes a heightened issue, particularly for women living at some distance from services and family.

Ageing men

The experience of ageing for men remains largely invisible in policy and practice terms. Data and research on men are often contextualised in relation to the differences between men and women (for example in terms of the differential mortality rates already discussed in this chapter). This comparative research tends to portray men in many respects as less 'well off' than women; for example, women are reported to be better at forming social networks and so men, in comparison, are regarded as potentially at risk of isolation and loneliness. While there is some research on ageing men and masculinity (e.g. Calasanti and King, 2007a), the experience of ageing men is relatively under-researched.

In terms of responses in practice, men appear to be poorly served. Women are more like to be widowed and to live longer than men, so men are often in the minority and attention to the needs of ageing men in, for example, care environments may not be well developed. Greater attention has been given to men who provide informal care to their partners (e.g. Davidson *et al.*, 2003; Calasanti and King, 2007a).

Ethnicity

In 2008 British minority ethnic groups comprised 9 per cent of England's population, with 3 per cent of people within those groups aged 65 and over. While the age structure of black and minority ethnic groups is still rather younger than that of the white majority population, this is slowly changing. Some ethnic minority groups are 'older' than others. For example, while 13 per cent of the black Caribbean population was aged 65 and over in 2008, this applied to only 4 per cent of the Pakistani population and 2 per cent of the black African population (Age Concern, 2008). Such differences can be explained by variations in migration history, gender composition and mortality.

Patterns of migration also point to different experiences for groups of black and minority ethnic people. The experience of ageing must be underpinned by an awareness of diversity rather than assumptions about homogeneity. While there are parallels in needs and aspirations between elders from the majority group, there exist specific areas of difference and/or concern arising from language and culture, faith and the consequences and experience of racism. Research on outcomes valued by older people (Glendinning, 2007) highlighted that while older people from a diverse range of backgrounds value similar outcomes, the priority given to specific outcomes is likely to be influenced by, for example, the importance attached to meeting religious and cultural needs. Black and minority elders are often disadvantaged in knowing what services are available and are likely to avoid services that they perceive as being culturally inappropriate or geared around the needs of the majority group (PRIAE, 2005). Although it is likely that minority ethnic groups will benefit from increased personalisation of services in order that they may access care and support according to their need and preference, specific outreach strategies and support may be required to ensure equal access (Newbigging and Lowe, 2005).

Health

A further area of difference between older people is in relation to their health; such diversity will increasingly be significant for social workers to appreciate as health becomes a major area in assessment, and inter-professional practice with health care professionals is a key ingredient in social work practice.

Point for reflection

- Why might older people define their heath more positively than more 'objective' measures of their physical health might indicate?
- How do you define health and wellbeing? How might definitions of health and wellbeing change at different points on the life course?

Those in the older population vary considerably in terms of their health. However, most older people have one or more long-standing illnesses. In 2006, 63 per cent of people aged 65–74 and 70 per cent of those aged 75 and over reported living with a long-standing illness (ONS, 2010). Of medication prescribed in the UK, 45 per cent is for people aged 65 and over and 36 per cent of those aged 75 and over take four or more prescribed drugs (SCIE, 2005). Nevertheless, when older people are asked to describe their overall health state, a high proportion tend to rate their health as either good or very good. This is because older people tend to define health using a wider range of criteria than the absence of illness or disability; being able to carry on with their usual roles and responsibilities and do what they want to do are fundamental considerations for older people in their assessment of health and wellbeing.

Nevertheless, health problems do affect a larger number of people in later life. For example, Action on Hearing Loss (formerly the Royal National Institute for Deaf People; 2009) indicates that 6.5 million people over 60 in the UK have age-related hearing loss. Among people aged 70 and over, 71.5 per cent have some kind of hearing loss and 50 per cent have moderate or serious hearing impairment. Visual impairment is also more likely to become an issue as people age. Among the oldest age groups, the Royal National Institute of Blind People suggests that 50 per cent of people live with sight loss, caused most commonly by age-related conditions such as macula degeneration, glaucoma, cataracts and diabetic retinopathy (RNIB, 2010).

Practice focus

Deaf awareness?

Katya is an older woman living with her husband of 50 years. Originally from the Ukraine, she has lived in a small town in the West Midlands for over 30 years, where she has built up a large network of friends through her work, church activities and other hobbies. She has one daughter and two grandchildren. Katya was diagnosed with presbycusis (age-related hearing loss) and was prescribed hearing aids.

Over the past few months Katya's mood and behaviour have changed. She has become less sociable and seems to go out less often and to fewer places. Her friends have noticed that she avoids going to places where there is a lot of background noise (for example coffee shops, restaurants, the pub). She confided in a close friend that she feels foolish because she cannot hear in environments with lots of background noise and increasingly feels as if she cannot take part in conversations. She believes that people have started to exclude her or that they tend to shout at her if she does not hear the first time. She is embarrassed when she cannot hear and feels foolish when people shout at her. Katya has found her hearing aids difficult to adjust to and was disappointed that they did not solve the hearing problems she experienced. She has come to the conclusion that these difficulties must be a part of old age and that there is nothing she can do about them.

The proportion of older people who report long-term illness or disability that restricts daily activities increases with age. The impact of conditions such as arthritis on mobility is well known, with an incidence in women of approximately 250 in 1000 of the population aged between 65 and 74, and 113 in 1000 in the population of men (Arthritis Care, 2007). Mental ill-health may also be an experience in older age; this may be because a person has had long-standing mental health needs and has aged with them, or because they have developed mental ill-health in later life. While dementia, for example, can affect people through the whole life course, its prevalence is much higher in older age. Social workers working with older people will inevitably encounter those with cognitive impairment associated with dementia and so it is imperative that practitioners have a sound grasp of the knowledge and skills required to work positively with people living with dementia.

While depression can affect anyone through the life course, it is more common in older people than in any other age group. The Mental Health Foundation (2010) estimates that 10–15 per cent of older people living in the community show symptoms of depression, but this figure rises to approximately 40 per cent when considering older people living in care homes (Eisses *et al.*, 2005). Many people living with dementia may also have depression, which often goes undiagnosed in these circumstances. The potential for age-based discrimination in the context of mental health is an issue that is of concern to older people affected, their families and practitioners (Kings Fund, 2005). This has considerable implications for social work practice given the importance ascribed to challenging structural oppression and discrimination.

Messages from research

The psychosocial impact of vision loss on older people (Nyman et al., 2010)

This research reviewed 174 research papers to assess the evidence of psychosocial impacts on older people with vision loss. The findings indicate the following:

- Older people with vision loss are more at risk of reporting symptoms of depression and lower mental health, and being diagnosed with clinical depression, than are their sighted peers.
- The risk of depressive symptoms is higher in those with worse visual functioning.
- Social functioning is likely to be reduced in individuals with vision loss, but not social network size or social activity.
- Interventions that address psychosocial needs directly are more effective than rehabilitation that addresses them indirectly through instrumental support.

Implications for practice

In conjunction with rehabilitation, emotional needs should be considered, which might include referring the person for counselling or group support services in addition to informal support. The authors conclude that the evidence base is at present insufficient to recommend a particular form of emotional support.

Class and income

In old age the effect of class and income is amplified through retirement. Class influences lifestyles in older age. Additionally, the lower the socioeconomic status of an older person, the more likely it is that they will experience ill-health. ONS (2010) highlights that inequalities in health persist, with 30 per cent of those aged 50 and over living in social rented accommodation in England and Wales reporting a long-term condition. Men and women in social classes III manual and IV and V are more likely than those in non-manual social classes to have a mental health problem.

Similarly, research findings suggest that mental health problems in later life tend to decrease with increasing income, thus areas of wealth and prosperity see a lower prevalence of mental health problems (Asthana and Halliday, 2006). Contributing to an occupational pension, owning property, accruing savings and retiring on a high income (Thompson, 1995) will also influence financial resources in later life. In the past 30 years the increasing importance of a non-state pension has resulted in a growing inequality between those who have and those who do not have occupational pensions. Redundancy, unemployment, care for dependent children or adults all have a significant impact on the ability of people to accrue such a pension. Low public pensions are increasingly meaning a reliance on means-tested top-up benefits, with a quarter of all older people in Britain dependent on Pensioner Credit, or entitled to it but not claiming it (www.poverty.org.uk).

Location

The socioeconomic and demographic factors discussed above divide the older population in a number of ways. In addition, the experience of ageing is also affected by diversity in where older people live, for example between rural and urban environments and between different countries. Although it is beyond the scope of this book to highlight global differences in ageing, placing Britain relative to other countries does throw some light on the relative position of older people in the country today.

The majority of the world's population of older people (61 per cent) live in poorer countries, many where life expectancy remains below 50. For example, life expectancy at birth in Afghanistan, the Central Republic of Africa and the Democratic Republic of Congo is 48 (www.who.int/imp, 2009). In 2004 about 1.2 billion people globally were living on an income of less than $1 per day and about 100 million of those are older than 60 (Petersen, 2004).

Trends in Britain reflect more general trends at a European level. Low fertility levels and extended longevity mean that the EU population is ageing, particularly those over age 80. At the same time, the population of working age is dwindling; in 2001 the old age dependency ratio (the population aged 65 and over as a percentage of the working age population 15–64) had risen to 24.6 per cent, an increase of 4 per cent in 10 years (Eurostat, 2002). This continuing trend will have implications for social policy in all EU member states and, even with the more balanced demographics of the new accession states, will remain a significant issue on the migration agenda.

Moving from a European level to a country level, significant differences in the experiences of ageing are found in urban and rural areas. For some older people there is a choice of migrating to warmer climates of other countries or to the seaside.

Older people living in rural areas may face a lack of services and difficulties accessing any limited provision. The experience of those living in rural areas is influenced by factors such as poor transport, centralisation of services and resources, and lack of service provision (Scharf and Bartlam, 2006). Older people living in rural communities may express need in terms of loneliness and isolation, accentuated by depopulation, the purchase of local houses as second homes and holiday houses, and the loss of personal networks through geographical mobility and bereavement. Clearly, there is a need for care and support services to develop in the context of familiarity with the area and the population that they serve. While it may seem common sense to focus resources on centralised and traditional day care for older people in the nearest town, for those living in rural settings travelling to town for a few hours may feel unfamiliar, stressful and unnecessary, as well as having little to do with their interests and aspirations. There is thus a need to reconsider traditional approaches to providing support services for older people that respond positively to their needs and aspirations by, for example, supporting or encouraging the development of local resources or small-scale community projects.

Ageing in the inner city, however, does not necessarily mean that older people will have easy access to a range of support services. Many older people live in deprived inner-city areas with poor resources. In their study of ageing in three deprived inner-city areas, Scharf *et al.* (2005) highlighted that 34 per cent of respondents identified a lack of social clubs or community centres for older people in the neighbourhood. Other locations that superficially appear to be satisfactory may also not meet the needs of older people; urban regeneration, for example, can create environments suitable for professionally mobile couples but result in facilities that are important to other citizens exiting the area. Suburban areas may also suffer from poor transport links; out-of-town shopping centres may cause the demise or deterioration of more traditional town centre shopping areas that are accessible to older people without public transport. The World Health Organisation promotes the recognition of 'age-friendly' cities, which it defines as having an inclusive and accessible urban environment that promotes 'active ageing' (World Health Organisation, 2010).

It is clear that the experience of ageing is influenced at least in part by where people age. Research has demonstrated consistent health inequalities among older people by region and area. For example, mortality rates differ by geographical region, with the highest life expectancies in the South East and South West of England and the lowest in Scotland and the North West and North East of England. At a local area level, the borough of Kensington and Chelsea heads the highest life expectancy at age 65, with males expected to live a further 23.7 years and females a further 26.5 years. Glasgow City had the lowest life expectancy at age 65, with men being expected to live a further 13.9 years and women 17.6 years (Nelson, 2006). Similarly, Scotland consistently displays the highest rates of chronic heart disease and South England the lowest.

Location may also be an important factor encouraging movement in later life. For several decades, retirement migration has been a feature of British society. Typically, areas where the proportion of people above retirement age is higher than 20 per cent are concentrated along coastal areas of the country, for example Cornwall (Tomassini, 2005). Some local authority districts such as Christchurch in Dorset and Rother in East Sussex have a population profile that includes over 30 per cent of people over retirement age. Increasingly, wealthier older people are moving abroad to places such as Southern Spain and Italy to savour the benefits of the climate. However, this is also likely to lead to a number of potential problems in respect of future welfare provision.

Long distances come into sharp focus for ethnic communities engaged in transnational caring. Increased transnationalism means that it is necessary to reconsider the ways in which we define households along the ideas of co-residency and physical unity and to take into account the possibility of physical separation. A scholarship of transnational caring – how caring is achieved in spite of geographical distance – is developing in recognition of these newer forms of caring (Estes *et al.*, 2003). Schiller *et al.* (1992: 5) describe such people as 'transmigrants', who link their country of origin and their new country of settlement, sustaining familial, social and economic relationships and taking actions such as decision making across boundaries. An awareness of the potential complexity of family ties, care and support arrangements for people from minority ethnic backgrounds is clearly a critical issue for social work practice.

Housing and communities

In considering issues in ageing that have particular relevance for social work, housing is a key factor. National policy is underpinned by the principle of enabling older people to retain their independence and autonomy and, wherever possible, to remain in their own homes. Housing has a crucial role to play in this equation as people 'age in place'. Housing conditions and housing tenure also play significant roles in the quality of life. The Joseph Rowntree Foundation (Garwood, 2010) highlights the importance of good-quality housing to health and wellbeing and the compelling case for integrated inter-professional work between social workers, health practitioners and housing providers. There is great diversity in housing wealth, with 15 per cent of older home owners being income and equity poor, and 5 per cent being both income rich and equity rich. Further diversity in housing can be seen in relation to ethnicity, housing status and rural/urban location (Heywood *et al.*, 2002).

While the majority of homes are in reasonable condition, some poor housing remains and there are signs that new problems are emerging, particularly for older and low-income, long-term resident home owners and private tenants. The English Housing Conditions Survey (Department for Communities and Local Government, 2009) notes that 84 per cent of older people reported to live in non-decent housing reside in private-sector housing. While the number of younger home owners is reducing, home ownership among older people is high at around 75 per cent, 84 per cent for people aged between 60 and 70 (Adams, 2010). Low-income home owners may experience significant difficulties in maintaining their homes, especially if they live in older housing that is more likely to need costly repairs and adaptations.

In the past, sheltered housing has been seen as a viable alternative for older people who may identify a need for some support. The initial intentions of sheltered provision to provide companionship and community life as well as enable independence backfired, however, with an increasing tendency for tenants to rely on the warden or to need greater levels of support than sheltered housing was able to give. More recently, the development of 'extra care sheltered housing' (ECSH) has grown to a provision of over 30 000 units of extra care in England in 2006. Croucher *et al.* (2006), in a detailed literature review on ECSH, found that residents attached value to the combination of independence and security; however, some differences of opinion between tenants and support staff as to what constituted independence were noted. Croucher's research concluded that while ECSH provided some important opportunities for companionship and support, very frail people and those with sensory and cognitive impairments remained consistently on the margins of social engagement. It remains to be seen in the longer term whether ECSH offers older people with high support needs a home for life or whether the need to move to a care home continues to be an issue as older people's care needs become more complex.

There are a number of gaps in research exploring appropriate models of housing provision. For example, there remains a need to continue to examine ways to support people living with dementia to remain in their own homes with appropriate support. The research on extra care housing also needs to be developed in order to produce robust measures of wellbeing outcomes (Croucher *et al.*, 2006; Vallely *et al.*, 2006).

Retirement communities have seen a recent major expansion in the UK. Essentially, retirement villages offer, in various forms, independent housing with leisure and community facilities and may include care services, including in some schemes nursing home care.

Separate from housing but of increasing significance is the work on the 'meaning of home'. 'Home' has been regarded as a domestic setting with all its associated memories, but less attention has been applied to this principle once older people have entered residential care.

The significance of home is, however, taking precedence in housing policy to encourage initiatives for people to remain in their own homes. The use of technology is starting to have an impact on housing provision for disabled people too. There have been a number of initiatives in this arena that assist older people. Three are briefly outlined below.

- Lifetime homes to meet the needs of all the family are of increasing significance, initially termed 'multi-generational housing' to promote the theme of 'home for life' (Kelly, 2001: 57). It is claimed that such housing enables greater mobility through larger space, better standards, planning and fixtures, while locating such housing in accessible areas will also improve a feeling of neighbourhood community. For example, one of the criteria inside the home is space for a wheelchair to turn in all ground-floor rooms, the sitting room to be at entrance level and sufficient space downstairs for a bed or the conversion of a room into a bedroom. Contrary to the universal myth that all older people could downsize in later life, many older people will need as much space as earlier in their lives to maintain their lifestyles (Appleton, 2002).

- For existing old homes, 'Care and Repair' or 'Staying Put' schemes have been initiated. Resale value is an issue with many owners in terms of whether they will be able to market a property with a stair lift and other adaptations (Adams, 2010).
- Assistive technology has been installed to facilitate independent living and, for example, support risk taking and risk-management strategies. Examples include longer-term traditional devices such as social alarms and alarm pull-cord systems. More recently, automatic lighting, temperature-monitoring devices and medicine monitoring have become readily available. Movement-activated technology using passive infra-red devices (switching lights on and off automatically in response to movement), automatic taps and route-finding and orientation devices have proved to be of considerable help to older people, for example with cognitive impairment.

How older people use and perceive spaces in their communities is crucial for their quality of life. A study by Scharf et al. (2002) illustrated the significance of environment, indicating that older people who live in deprived neighbourhoods are more vulnerable to crime than those living in other neighbourhoods. Of the people participating in their survey, 40 per cent had been victims of one or more types of crime in the two years prior to the interview. While crime surveys repeatedly show that older people are relatively unlikely to be victims of crime, this study showed otherwise, particularly for ethnic minorities. Vulnerability to crime is linked to poverty and social inequality, as many studies over the years have suggested (Hough, 1995; Silverman and Della-Giustina, 2001; Scharf et al., 2002).

Older people's perceptions of place were also affected by their experience of crime or fear of crime. Waters and Neale (2010) found in qualitative research with older people that personal safety concerns were overwhelmingly related to the social connotations of specific community locations. This meant that participants indicated social fears involving concern about declines in their own communities, as well as a more generalised belief in the decline in standards in wider society.

Transportation in terms of walking, driving and use of the public transport system are crucial issues for many older people. Older people can be excluded from transport systems either financially, temporally (unable to get to activities at night), personally or spatially (unable to get to destinations). The goal of transport policy should be to offer all members of society safe, satisfactory and environmentally friendly transportation resources at the lowest possible socioeconomic cost, while at the same time integrating those with functional impairments into all parts of society. To make public transport attractive, it must be adapted to the needs of travellers. The design of public transport must proceed from a holistic perspective and presuppose that people have very different needs and preferences when they travel. This implies a demand for high trip frequency, efficiency and good information about travel options, combined with high-level service and an accessible outdoor environment with short distances to bus stops and train stations. An 'age-friendly' city is one that facilitates active participation, sustains independence and reduces isolation (Help the Aged, 2007). These factors must be underpinned by accessible and affordable transport that is reliable and safe to use, as well as being inclusive to older people who have more complex mobility, health and sensory needs.

The circumstance of older people who are vulnerable to homelessness or who are homeless are generally under-recognised, a fact that is reflected in the lack of comprehensive statistical evidence showing the extent of the problem. The UK Coalition on Older Homelessness (www.olderhomelessness.org.uk, 2004) defines older homeless people as 'those who are 50 plus and are sleeping rough or living in appropriate temporary accommodation, or are at risk of homelessness'. Older homeless people are a marginalised group who remain invisible in policy debates and the development of service provision (Pannell *et al.*, 2002). Again, this perhaps highlights the ways in which our stereotyped assumptions of ageing and the experiences that older people may encounter inform our thinking and behaviour. It is the case, however, that older homeless people often have very complex needs as well as considerable support and occupational needs (Wilcock, 2006). As an example, older people discharged from prison are likely to have complex needs in terms of their resettlement, which are very likely to include insecure domicile or homelessness. Recoop (2010) highlights that older people are often separated from support networks and communities as a result of their imprisonment or offending behaviour, which means that they often have very few resources from which to draw support on release.

Care homes

The history of residential care has been well documented (Means and Smith, 1985, 1998; Phillips, 1992; Means et al., 2003; 2008). Of women aged over 65, 6 per cent live in communal establishments such as care homes, compared to 3 per cent of men aged 65 and over (ONS, 2010). This figure rises to 23 per cent for women aged 85 and over and 12 per cent of men, which reflects the gender difference in mortality as well as the likelihood that women's potential access to caring resources will be depleted by widowhood and greater longevity. It will perhaps remain the case that for some people with the most complex needs, a collective care establishment such as a nursing home may be an appropriate housing option. However, social policy is increasingly directed towards older people receiving support at home so that they may remain at home if that is their choice.

If this aspiration is to become a reality, then there are complex issues to be overcome in terms of the attitudes that informal and formal carers may have about the 'best' place for an older person with complex needs to live, alongside a requirement to develop comprehensive support for older people with complex needs so that they receive reliable and appropriate home-based care and support. It remains the case, for example, that large numbers of older people are admitted to residential care straight from hospital (CSCI, 2007), which points to a greater need for opportunities for rehabilitation, intermediate treatment and ongoing assessment as well as comprehensive support services for older people in their own homes. This raises complex issues about affording the current cost of 24-hour live-in care for older people against the current cost of residential care (the latter, in most cases, being cheaper). It remains unlikely that a resource allocation system (RAS) would allocate sufficient funds for an older person to purchase sleep-in or waking care through the night in their own home, especially on a long-term basis.

Social support

In studies of the family and the community life of older people, the role of the family in supporting older people is central (Wenger, 1984; Phillipson *et al.*, 2001). Similarly, older people themselves play significant reciprocal roles within their families, spanning, among other things, care giving, financial assistance and emotional support. Friends are also important, particularly for those without family (Phillipson *et al.*, 2001). In communities friends also play important roles as citizens or volunteers. When older people are asked about who is important in their lives, family and friends are rated highly; less so are community members such as vicars; in contrast, formal support services such as health and social workers are inconsequential in the lives of the majority of older people (Phillipson *et al.*, 2001).

It is estimated that each week, around a quarter of families with children under 15 use grandparents to provide child care (Age Concern, 2004). Grandparents are a potentially crucial source of support for children who are looked after. Research exploring the circumstances of 270 looked-after children found that 45 per cent of kin carers were grandparents. From this sample, 31 per cent of carers identified that they were living with a long-term illness or disability and 75 per cent indicated that they were experiencing financial hardship (Farmer and Meyers, 2005).

Providing care is also time consuming, with 1.7 million carers devoting at least 20 hours a week to caring and 855 000 of these spending over 50 hours in this role. Consequently, the impact on carers' employment can be severe. In the Carers UK survey (Carers UK, 2010), around six out of ten carers had given up work to provide care. The consequences of the loss of income and pension accrual for women in terms of providing security in their own old age can therefore be significant (Evandrou and Glaser, 2003).

There are a number of further factors in care giving that have an impact on the experiences for both carer and care recipient, such as the history of the past relationship and the quality of that relationship (the relationship may be based on years of abuse between father and child, with the roles of abuser and abused now reversed); prognosis and trajectory of the illness or condition requiring care; and the carer's attitude (Nolan *et al.*, 1998).

One of the difficulties in establishing the number of carers in the population is the inconsistency in the definition of a 'carer', both in research studies and in the census. Census figures have varied between 6.8 million (1991) and 5.2 million (2001). The current census definition (2001) asks if 'you provide unpaid personal help for a friend or family member with a long-term illness, health problem or disability'. Respondents are asked to include problems that are due to old age. Personal help is defined as including assistance with basic tasks such as eating or dressing. Unpaid carers, generally spouses, other family members, friends and others in the community, are usually designated under the term 'informal carer', although this is misleading as there is little that is 'informal' about this role. On the other hand, those grouped under 'formal' carers are paid and are often perceived as part of the low-waged, low-skilled social care workforce. Efforts to raise the profile and professional standing of social care workers have been considerable, but remuneration for this group remains low and often around the national minimum wage.

Carers UK (2008) suggests that as many as 1.5 million people over 60 provide informal care. Older people who provide informal care are more likely to have health needs themselves, as well as being more likely to provide co-residential care. This means that care is not necessarily delimited by, for example, geographical separation and so co-resident carers are more likely to provide care over 24 hours, as well as being more likely to assist with personal and intimate care as well as supervision and monitoring overnight.

Conclusion: Implications for social work

The diverse situations and heterogeneity of older people provide a backdrop to social work. It is crucial to acknowledge the diversity in social, cultural, economic, financial, political, gender, generational and ethnic circumstances, among others. This collage of circumstances and experience also has a temporal dimension, as present circumstances are shaped by a lifetime of events, relationships, economic and social circumstances as well as class, gender, ethnicity, race and location.

Social workers meet older people from all lifestyles through their personal and professional relationships, yet they are more likely to work with those who experience poverty, ill-health, depression, dementia and unresolved traumas from earlier years, along with those in greatest need. It is imperative that social workers place their work in context and do not view older people from a negative and ageist perspective.

Given that most older people do not need social workers or come into contact with them, why is social work with older people important? What are the reasons for social work and what is the remit of the social worker in the lives of older people? Chapter 2 turns to why social work has a distinct role and contribution to play in the lives of older people.

Putting it into practice

1 Think about an older person you know. How does their experience differ from yours? How have gender, class, income, culture and location influenced their experiences in later life? You may find it helpful to interview them about significant life events and their experience of later life.
2 Investigate a cross-section of newspapers covering the main news items of the week. To what extent are older people evident in the news? What images and situations are portrayed in the media? How can these images be challenged or promoted?

Further resources

Carers UK (2008) *Carers' Policy Briefing: The National Strategy for Carers*, London: Carers UK, http://www.carersuk.org/Professionals/ResourcesandBriefings/Policybriefings, accessed 7 September 2011.
A comprehensive review of the economic, practical and psychosocial implications of providing informal care.

Evans, M. and Whittaker, A. (2010) *Sensory Awareness and Social Work*, Exeter: Learning Matters.
An introductory text for readers interested in learning more about sensory impairment and issues for practice with people who have sensory impairment.

Phillips, J. E., Ajrouch, K. J. and Hillcoat-Nalletamby, S. (2011) *Key Concepts in Social Gerontology*, Bristol: Policy Press.
An accessible guide to gerontological concepts, knowledge and research.

Action on Hearing Loss (formerly RNID), www.actiononhearingloss.org.uk
Lots of useful practical information, research and policy response documents on all matters relating to hearing loss.

Arthritis Care, www.arthritis.org.uk
 Information about the many types of arthritis, including a lot of useful downloadable information sheets about living with arthritis, as well as information on current research, policy and practice.

Royal National Institute of Blind People, www.rnib.org.uk
 Contains information on research, practical information, pages for carers and supporters and information about support groups and services.

CHAPTER 2

The case for social work with older people

CHAPTER OVERVIEW
- The context for social work with older people is potentially diverse and wide-ranging.
- Social work with older people involves working in complex areas of practice.
- Most older people do not use personal social services.
- Many conditions that are more prevalent in older age are traditionally under-recognised or under-researched (for example depression in older age; dementia).
- A critical approach to practice may help to manage some of the complexities and uncertainties inherent in social work practice.

Introduction

Chapter 1 outlined the diverse experiences of later life and the importance of social workers understanding the contexts in which ageing takes place. Most people do not need or come into contact with a social worker and live their lives without intervention from social services. However, a minority of older people and their carers will need to draw on social work skills. This chapter outlines some of the reasons for social work with older people.

Social workers also need to understand why they practise in particular ways and the chapter concludes by exploring frameworks for social work with older people, such as the importance of theory, knowledge-based practice and critical practice. Just as important is the legislative, policy and organisational context, which is further discussed in Chapter 3.

Older people and personal social services

The myth that ageing is inevitably a period of decline was challenged in Chapter 1. While people aged 85 and over are more likely to receive personal social services than any other age group, the need for personal social services in older age is by no means inevitable. There is a trend towards more hours of support being provided to fewer households, reflecting more intense forms of support for people deemed as being in the most severe need (ONS, 2010). This is partly because many older people remain in good health and maintain their ability to undertake their usual roles and responsibilities. It is also partly explained by the fact that spouses, family members and friends may provide care and support to those older people who need it, and do not seek the help of personal social services.

The current emphasis on responding to the most severe level of need means that older people with lower, but nevertheless significant, levels of need are ineligible for personal social services and either go elsewhere for support, find other ways to cope, or their needs go unmet (Tanner, 2010). There is a growing expectation that support should not be restricted to people with the most intensive needs, as this is argued to be a false economy and does not serve the community well, thus pointing towards a clearer commitment to preventative support (Department of Health, 2010a: 12). Despite the current government emphasis on local communities developing resources that meet local needs, critical questions remain about how an appropriate framework of preventative services and support will be developed.

There is a growing emphasis, especially in England, on individuals taking charge of their own care via personal budgets provided to eligible people so that they may make choices about the outcomes they want to achieve and the ways in which their individual needs and requirements are met. This policy development has clear implications for social work practice, including ensuring that people are able to access support services to manage their own budgets and to work with people to help them tailor support to meet their individual aspirations and outcomes. Nevertheless, provision of funds via direct payments will still be determined by identification of a person's needs via assessment, determining whether those needs fall within eligibility thresholds and identifiying each person's personal budget via the Resource Allocation System (RAS) (see Chapter 3).

Social work practice must also be underpinned by an awareness of the potential for age-based discrimination as a feature of everyday life for older people, for example in respect of poor practice and inadequate service delivery, underpinned by inappropriate attitudes and assumptions about older people as service users. As well as having a sound understanding of the causes of discrimination, social workers must develop skill in challenging poor practice and making good use of the legal frameworks, which are designed to protect people who may be vulnerable to discriminatory practice. A 'one size fits all approach' to social work with older people cannot be adequate in the context of such diversity of experiences and contexts in later life.

Complex life circumstances experienced by an older service user add further layers of intricacy to a social worker's own involvement and, indeed, her or his involvement with other agencies. This again highlights the importance of providing interventions that do the following:

- Tailor services to individual need and actively seek to enable an older person to build on their strengths, abilities and resources, rather than focusing on problems, dysfunctions and pathologies. Looking at the strengths of older people and the resilience they develop to multiple losses over their lifetime is a starting point for social work assessment.
- Plan and provide interventions aimed at alleviating the difficulties associated with the context and based on the needs and aspirations of the older person (for example, enabling an older person to talk about their bereavement and facilitate communication).
- Realise the potential for change in older people in terms of physical, mental and emotional health. Older people are often resilient in the face of severe difficulties.
- Evaluate the outcomes of services and interventions. Did your interventions do what they set out to do? Has the older person achieved goals and outcomes that were important and relevant to him/her? In what way has there been change, and to what extent?
- Mediate and advocate for older people (for example in respect of allocating resources and services; helping an older person attend and participate in a case conference or review meeting).
- Advocate for older people who, by virtue of the complexity of their needs, are most at risk of being marginalised or

depersonalised to the extent that their rights to good-quality care can be overlooked.
- Challenge health inequalities and contribute to developing policy and practice in health promotion.

We now turn to considering some of the reasons why social workers may work with older people.

Reasons for social work

Physical frailty

Social workers are likely to meet older people who are viewed as 'frail', through both physical disability and/or cognitive impairment. The major causes of ill-health in later life include cardiovascular diseases (stroke and coronary heart disease), cancers, arthritis, sensory impairment and cognitive impairment caused by dementia. Older people may also have to cope with several long-term conditions; the interactions between those conditions and their impact on wellbeing is an important consideration. Alongside physical morbidity, consideration must be given to the social circumstances and contexts in which older people experience long-lasting illness, their coping strategies and the resources and supports they have in place to assist in coping with deteriorating conditions. It is important, therefore, that social workers have an awareness of conditions that may most commonly affect older people along with some of the potential implications of living with those conditions. This is critical in terms of enabling social workers to engage positively and professionally with older people, so that older service users feel able to discuss their needs and challenges fully. Moreover, such a knowledge base, backed up by appropriate skills and values, will make a distinct contribution to inter-professional practice in multi-disciplinary settings.

Current social policy places considerable emphasis on the importance of achieving outcomes geared towards preserving independence, autonomy and self-determination (Department of Health, 2010a). These are important aspirations, and social work practice should always focus on enabling people to achieve their desired outcomes in a way that suits them. Nevertheless, there is also an important debate about the value that is placed on the concept of independence at the expense of other critical issues, such as an ethic of care and ensuring a person's dignity, especially when the person has complex needs. Lloyd (2004) questions the extent to which principles of choice and control can be stretched beyond the limits of possibility for people at the end of their life, for example. This raises important issues about the role that social workers play in advocating for older people who, by virtue of complex needs and ill-health, may struggle to assert themselves and who are likely to be at most risk of being marginalised and having their needs over-shadowed. A distinct contribution by social workers should be to ensure that people who are most vulnerable to being marginalised are able to access sensitive and appropriate support and assistance that takes account of their individual needs and aspirations.

Dementia

Older people may live with cognitive impairment for a number of reasons. They may experience long-term consequences for their cognition resulting from a stroke, for instance. Approximately 130 000 people each year have a stroke and stroke accounts for over 11 per cent of deaths in England and Wales annually (Stroke Association, 2011). Early recognition of stroke, together with specialist treatment, enhances the likelihood of survival and can reduce the impact of cognitive impairment following stroke (National Audit Office, 2005). A major stroke may result in a person living with dementia; vascular dementia is the second most common form of dementia in England, Wales and Scotland (National Audit Office, 2005).

There are some 750 000 people in the UK living with a form of dementia and it is expected that by 2051, 1.7 million people will have been diagnosed with dementia (Knapp and Prince, 2007). While dementia affects a significant minority of younger people, the incidence of dementia in older age is much more significant. It is estimated that one in six people over 80 years has a form of dementia.

Great strides have been made over the past two decades in raising the profile of the needs of people living with dementia; nevertheless, dementia care services have suffered from a history of neglect and it remains the case that experiences of stigma and poor, fragmented and at times ill-informed responses to requests for assistance and support are commonplace experiences for people living with dementia. Moreover, the evidence is that older people, particularly those living with dementia, are often over-medicated and given antipsychotic medication to manage symptoms that are perceived as challenging or intractable. Banerjee (2009) has high-lighted the extent of this issue and the urgent need to develop better responses to people with dementia, via for example psychosocial interventions and improved approaches to care and support. There is also compelling evidence that older people with dementia do not have access to well-developed interventions (for example psychoso-cial support) and this may have major consequences for the person's wellbeing and quality of life.

The National Dementia Strategy and subsequent updates to the strategy (Department of Health, 2009b, 2010a) highlight a number of key priorities aimed at addressing the history of neglect that has blighted dementia services. Current priorities focus on the following:

• Good-quality early diagnosis and intervention.
• Improved quality of care in general hospitals.
• Improved care for people with dementia who live in care homes.
• A reduction in the use of antipsychotic medication as a first-line response to what are perceived as 'challenging behaviours' and a corresponding growth in psychosocial interventions.

Social workers are likely to play a significant role in supporting people living with dementia through assessment, securing appro-priate support and coping with the challenges and transitions asso-ciated with the condition.

Depression

Older people may face a range of emotional and psychological challenges that they require help and support to manage. Social workers frequently meet older people who experience low morale because of disability and illness; who are bereaved or facing loss (either of people or loss associated with their own illness); who experience a shrinking network as a result of successive bereave-ments; or who are facing death or are dying. Depression may be caused by the experience of or difficulties in managing or coping with bereavement, loss and change and long-lasting illness. The RNIB, for example, reports that older people with sight loss are three times more likely to experience depression than people with good vision (RNIB, 2009). People may also become depressed as a result of untreated illness; it is easy to imagine, for instance, how unmanaged or untreated pain experienced over a period can result in a person feeling low and depressed. Such challenges can occur at any stage in the life course, but are more commonly associated with older age.

Medication (such as antibiotics, anti-Parkinsonian or anti-psychotic drugs) and their side effects can also be a cause of depression. At a practical level, this may be a major contributory factor in the high incidence of depression among older people living in care home environments, as they are more likely to be receiving medication for a range of illnesses and conditions. It is estimated that between 10 and 15 per cent of people over 65 have depression and this figure rises to over 40 per cent of older people who live in care homes (Royal College of Psychiatry, 2008). Moreover, people living at home who are susceptible to loneliness are characterised by similar factors to those commonly associated with depression, including poor health rating, health worse in old age than expected and mental morbidity (Victor *et al.*, 2005).

It remains the case that older people do not come close to receiving consistent diagnosis, treatment, practical assistance and follow-up in depression; indeed, many people with depression receive no treatment at all (Royal College of Psychiatry, 2008). The fragmented response evidences direct discrimination in terms of poor access to counselling, psychosocial and other forms of help (Royal College of Psychiatry, 2008; Ilife, 2009).

Social workers have a potentially critical role to play in developing awareness of the risk factors for depression and assisting older people in seeking advice and support. Moreover, social workers who assist older people with securing services to meet their needs should be aware of the benefits of broader preventative strategies that reduce social isolation and enable older people to develop social and support networks. Skilled social workers should contribute to the leadership needed to promote cultural and attitudinal change to the all-too-often poor responses to mental health needs in later life.

Suicide

While death by suicide among older people remains at a relatively small percentage of the population, it constitutes a significant minority that should not be overlooked. Older people are more successful than any other age group at taking their own life and any attempt at suicidal behaviour or self-harm should be taken seriously and the person carefully assessed (Beeston, 2006; Tanner, 2010).

Risk factors for death by suicide among older people include clinical depression, poor physical health, social isolation and loneliness (Tanner, 2010). Older people who are at risk of dying by suicide may be overlooked because of ageist stereotypes that assume that older age will inevitably cause depression, anxiety and changes in behaviour. Prevention strategies imply a need for a much greater awareness of the possibility of an older person dying by suicide, as well as wider initiatives to combat stereotypes of ageing and stigma associated with mental health problems, and the building of positive social initiatives that build civic and social engagement among older people in the community (Beeston, 2006).

Alcohol misuse

As with any group in the population, older adults can also have problems with alcohol (Mental Health Foundation, 2010). The Royal College of Psychiatry suggests that 1 in 6 older men and 1 in 15 older women are drinking enough to harm themselves. Recent research by Foundation 66 (2009) suggested that 1 in 8 older people drinks more following retirement and uses alcohol to 'manage' depression, bereavement or isolation.

Our assumptions based on what older people 'do' may mean that we overlook problem drinking, or wrongly ascribe it to something else. These researches highlight the importance of developing a sound awareness and knowledge base surrounding the kinds of issues that may affect older people, as well as a reflexive approach to challenging our own assumptions and stereotypes about ageing and working with older people.

Care giving

The need to act as a carer can occur at any age, although the 'structural potential' (the likelihood of caring in relation to position in society) for care giving increases with age (Martin-Mathews and Keefe, 1995). Until the early 1990s, the crucial role that older women and men played in co-resident spouse care was virtually invisible in both research and policy terms. Arber and Ginn (1991) were the first to demonstrate, in their re-analysis of the General Household Survey, the contribution of older people in care provision, amounting to 35 per cent of the total volume of informal care to people aged 65 or over and nearly 50 per cent of co-resident care of older men and women. The contribution of older male spouses caring for their partners has continued and by the end of the twentieth century as many men as women cared for their spouse/partner (Hirst, 2001). Subsequent research has confirmed the sustained importance of co-resident care (e.g. Rowlands and Parker, 1998; Hirst, 2001) and the Office of National Statistics (2010a) highlighted that the number of older people providing care in excess of 35 hours per week has steadily increased.

Despite recognition that caring takes place in the context of a relationship and that the relationship inevitably informs the way in which care is constructed and experienced, research that includes the perspectives of care giver and care recipient continues to be relatively rare. In terms of long-lasting relationships, it is important to develop an understanding of the meanings that couples may ascribe to their relationship and how those meanings influence their experience of emerging from long-lasting illness (Ray, 2006).

The context of elderly spouse care is distinguished by a number of features. First, co-resident care provides opportunities for intense forms of care giving, as it is not limited by, for example, geographical distance. Co-resident care is most likely to consist of activities such as the provision of health interventions, care of a personal or intimate nature and supervisory and monitoring roles (Pickard *et al.*, 2000).

Practice focus

Care for a long-term partner

Saul Jenkins has been married to his wife Ada, for over 55 years. Ada was diagnosed with Alzheimer's disease approximately four years ago. Initially, she managed to carry on with many of her usual activities, with a little support from Saul. More recently, however, her health has deteriorated. Her mobility has decreased because she has arthritis and, together with her cognitive difficulties, she becomes very anxious about moving out of the house. Sometimes Ada has difficulty finding her way around inside the home, so Saul feels that he must be with her all of the time to keep her safe. This means that he relies on their daughter to help with shopping and paying the bills and he rarely feels confident enough to go out and leave his wife at home – even with care from another person. Ada sometimes wakes up at night and so Saul gets up to be with her. He is helping with all of her personal care.

The couple can afford a private cleaner who comes in three times a week and cleans the house, washes and irons. Saul tries to get into the garden, but with mixed success. Sometimes Ada will happily let him go into the garden and will sit and watch him work, but at other times she becomes distressed and afraid.

Saul and Ada have been to the doctor's to ask if anything can be done about Ada's poor mobility, but the doctor has indicated that it is 'just her age'. Saul is very afraid to have any involvement from social services, as his neighbour of 40 years had a social worker visit her and she subsequently moved into a care home. Saul is very afraid that he will be separated from Ada if he involves anyone else and so struggles on alone. His daughter is very worried about them both and feels that they should talk to social services to see what help they might be able to offer them.

- What do you think might be the main issues and concerns when caring for a long-term partner?
- How would you approach talking with Saul and Ada about their situation?
- What would you have to consider when working with a long-term couple?

Informal care in the context of non-heterosexual relationships remains substantially under-investigated. There are likely to be around 57 000 gay and lesbian people in the UK with a diagnosis of dementia who are supported by partners, family and friends (Price, 2008). Nevertheless, despite the significance of the population, the needs of gay and lesbian people remain almost invisible.

Older people may also provide care and support to disabled children into adulthood and, indeed, provide life-long care and support. Research by Janick et al. (2010) examined the role of parent carers for adult offspring with Down's syndrome and with a diagnosis of dementia. Their research highlighted that parents were engaged in long-term or lifetime caring for their son or daughter. Older parents looked for support in terms of advice and assistance to cope with their son or daughter's changing cognitive abilities and behaviour, but did not exhibit any significant evidence of burden or carer-related ill-health. Tobin (1996) has argued that this level of positive adjustment relates to parent carers being 'adaptive copers'; that is, they have, over their lifetime, had time to adjust to and cope with the demands and expectations of providing very long-term care for their adult offspring.

Older people with learning disabilities are likely to experience the same potential challenges as anyone else, such as joint stiffness, pain and reduced mobility caused by arthritis, or other long-term conditions such as diabetes. It is critical that social workers are sensitive to conditions that may have an impact on the wellbeing of people with learning disabilities as they age. This may involve having a detailed understanding of the ways in which a person communicates distress or pain; accessing tools or strategies and the skill to aid in communication; and advocating as necessary to ensure that the person gets fair and equal treatment. People with Down's syndrome are especially susceptible to developing Alzheimer's disease and it is estimated that 50 per cent of people with Down's syndrome in their fifties will experience cognitive impairment caused by dementia (www.downs-syndrome.org.uk).

Point for reflection

- In what ways might stereotyped assumptions and discrimination have an impact on an older person with learning difficulties in gaining fair and equal access to services?
- In what ways can age-based discrimination influence the lives of older people?
- In what ways do you think other forms of discrimination (e.g. gender-based discrimination) might impact on the experience of ageing?

Hospital discharge

Hospital social work is a key area of practice with older people. It involves working in a multi-disciplinary team to treat an older person, assess their needs, plan further interventions such as inter-mediate care and plan their discharge. Ultimately, the team is responsible for ensuring that appropriate support is in place for a safe and secure discharge from hospital. Annual statistics (2009–10) show an increase in hospital admissions across the life course, with a 66 per cent increase in admission rates for people aged over 75 when compared with figures for the period 1999–2000 (www.ic.nhs.uk).

Even in the fast-paced atmosphere of a hospital, social workers can play a crucial role in forming a relationship with an older person to ensure that their needs and aspirations are identified and remain central to planning care and support needs. The social work knowledge and skill base means that social workers can work effectively with complex systems, including family members, and negotiate when there are differences of opinion about what should happen to an older person following their discharge from hospital. Research demonstrates the ways in which an older person with high support needs may have their wishes and aspirations disregarded (Blood, 2010), so it is critical that social workers consider their role as advocate for such a person when necessary.

Social workers practising within a multidisciplinary team must be clear about the knowledge and skills they bring to the team. Lymbery (2005: 122) has argued that social workers have to ensure that they are respected for their practice abilities in a health care setting, as well as expecting to 'struggle to carve out a role within health settings'. This comment reflects the challenge of working in an inter-professional context where traditional power hierarchies have assumed the dominance of a medical model and medical practitioners. Nevertheless, the requirement to collaborate across professions remains critical and social work can make a vital contribution to providing services that do not compromise the dignity and personhood of older people. Recent reports by the Ombudsman's Office have highlighted the unacceptable consequences for older people in hospital who have been depersonalised to the extent that their treatment constitutes abusive practice:

> The theme of poor communication and thoughtless action extends to discharge arrangements, which can be shambolic and ill-prepared, with older people being moved without their family's knowledge or consent. Clothing and other possessions are often mislaid along the way. One 82-year-old woman recalled how, on being discharged from hospital after minor surgery, she was frightened and unsure of how to get home. She asked the nurse to phone her daughter. '*He told me this was not his job*', she said. (Parliamentary and Health Service Ombudsman, 2011: 9)

Moving into a care home

It is estimated that approximately 468 000 care-home places exist for older people in the UK (Age Concern, 2007). Nevertheless, as we discussed in Chapter 1, the number of older people who live in care homes is relatively small. Current social policy emphasises the need to develop support services and effective community resources to ensure that older people can remain at home and are not 'forced' to move to a care home simply because there are inadequate services in place. Evidence certainly demonstrates that older people may move into a care home because of a range of factors that have little to do with their personal choice. Transition to a care home may be precipitated by the following:

- A crisis that is reinforced by a lack of appropriate community services and difficulties gaining access to potentially suitable services (Taylor and Donnelly, 2006).
- A lack of other options (Challis and Hughes, 2002).
- Poor understanding of the needs of people with dementia and a lack of appropriate services to cater for those needs (Vallelly *et al.*, 2006).
- Lack of clarity about the objectives of an intervention and rationing taking priority over other aspects of intervention (McDonald, 2010).
- An imperative to discharge the person before their potential for rehabilitation and a return home have been fully assessed or considered (CSCI, 2005).

Messages from research

Older people with high support needs (Blood, 2010)

A review of available evidence concerning the needs of older people with high support needs – including people living in care homes – highlights a number of critical factors that constitute significant barriers to older people participating in decision making at all levels:

- Low expectations of older people in terms of their capabilities and aspirations.
- An over-focus on the needs of the organisation to manage resources and determine eligibility at the expense of person-centred assessment, interventions and support.
- The impact of age-based discrimination.
- Poor development of creative and comprehensive communication strategies to enable people with communication difficulties to ensure their voice is heard.
- A lack of collective 'voice' for older people with high support needs.

Bowers *et al.* (2009) examined the experiences and aspirations of older people living in care homes and paint a bleak picture of the poor quality of life for many older people with the most complex support needs. This research highlights the need for substantial culture change to improve the quality of life for older people. Summing up the evidence, the authors frame the need for older people to have a 'good life', which includes:

- People knowing and caring about you.
- The importance of belonging.
- Being able to contribute to family, social, community and communal life.
- Being valued for what you can do.
- Being treated as an equal and an adult.
- Feeling that personal routines and commitments are respected and accommodated.
- Feeling able to spend time positively.
- Retaining a sense of self and identity that includes being able to express views and feelings.
- Feeling positive and good about physical surroundings (shared and private spaces).
- Getting out and about. (Bowers *et al.*, 2009)

Gerontological social workers should have the necessary skills to ensure that older people with high support needs are able to express their aspirations about the way in which they wish to receive support and assistance. Moreover, social workers have a critical role to play in shaping responses to commissioning and developing support services for older people in their communities. This may mean working in an inter-professional context with, for example, housing associations and community organisations to develop a more creative range of housing support options, including support at home or in alternative housing. Critically, it should involve encouraging the meaningful participation of older people with high support needs in developing services or tailoring support to individual need. If an older person decides to move into a care home environment, they should have access to a reliable and consistent approach to monitoring and reviewing standards of care. Social workers should have a role to play in this area of practice.

Older people in prison

Although this issue may seem somewhat marginal to social work, older people are the fastest-growing section of the prison population and often have complex needs. Research on the needs of older people who are in prison and who have been released from prison remains sparse and there is no specific national policy regarding this group. In terms of complexity of need, it is known that 10 per cent of prisoners are aged over 50 and that 50 per cent of this group have an identified mental disorder. From the limited research we know that inequality, homelessness, institutionalisation and a lack of a role outside prison can perpetuate and encourage dependency, deny autonomy and lead to recidivism (Howse, 2003).

There is an argument for the development of services that specifically recognise the needs of older offenders in prison. Parker *et al.* (2007) argue that there is little clarity about who should provide routine social care for older prisoners. The Law Commission review (2011) indicated in its recommendations an intention to clarify what social care services should be available for people in prison who had need of such services. This means making sure that prisoners with health and social care needs have access to an appropriate level of service and support, and also that there is a recognition of potentially complex need (for example, a diagnosis of dementia) among older prisoners, including those for whom release is unlikely.

Bereavement and loss

Social work with older people is likely to involve working with people who have experienced bereavement and other forms of loss and are having to cope with the transitions associated with those losses. Very old people are likely to have experienced the loss of a number of key relationships through death. Despite the fact that older people demonstrate considerable resilience in the face of what may amount to multiple bereavements, social workers must be mindful of the potential impact such losses may have on a person's emotional and physical wellbeing.

Traditional approaches to loss and bereavement focused on the idea of 'letting go' or coming to terms with the loss of the deceased person. More recently, there has been a recognition that people do not necessarily grieve in a way that can conclude with coming to terms with loss. The 'dual process' model (Stroebe and Shut, 1999, 2001) highlights that a bereaved person is likely to experience grief at their loss, but can at the same time engage in restoration-type activities that can include choosing not to focus on their loss, distracting themselves by doing different things or avoiding their feelings. Working with people who have experienced bereavement and loss means recognising the diversity of ways in which people experience loss and how those experiences are shaped by individual biography and cultural and social meanings of loss.

End of life

The palliative care needs of older people have become more visible in the past decade, as have the factors that may prevent good palliative care. Key barriers are identified as the following:

- Access to general health care and palliative care services.
- Training of practitioners to recognise the needs of older people at the end of life.
- Encouraging a recognition of the value of older people and challenging direct or indirect discrimination that may prevent older people from getting the services they need.
- Ensuring a good link between health and social care services as well as general and specialist palliative care services (Froggatt, 2004).

There is now a better recognition of the importance of good-quality care for older people at the end of life. Recently this has included a growing awareness of the palliative care needs of older people living with dementia. Social workers are likely to be involved in practice with older people with long-standing, limiting illnesses and conditions, which Froggatt (2004) argues should lead to a reconceptualisation of end-of-life care to involve a recognition that older people with high support needs may be approaching the end of life, but that this is characterised by uncertainty and that it is important to continue to experience a life of quality.

The role of social work and social care has been explicitly examined in the National End of Life care programme (2010), which highlights the unique contribution of palliative care social work as an educative and consultative resource for mainstream services as well as in specialist services. The programme highlights the importance of raising awareness of the role of social work and social care in supporting people at the end of life, as well as strengthening the role of social work and maximising social work contributions to end-of-life care.

Safeguarding older adults

Safeguarding older adults is a critical area of practice for gerontological social workers. At the time of writing, there is no legislation that directly clarifies the obligation to investigate, assess and respond to allegations of abuse, mistreatment or neglect. The local authority guidance 'No Secrets' (Department of Health, 2000) serves as guidance to local authorities as the lead agency in responding to abuse, as well as identifying an expectation that strategic and policy planning to prevent and intervene in issues of abuse will be underpinned by a coordinated, multi-agency approach.

There have been persistent calls for specific legislation that makes clear the duty to investigate allegations or situations of abuse. At the time of writing, no specific law exists to deal with the matter of safeguarding and protection. However, the Law Commission (2011) reported its recommendations on the current legislative arrangements for adult care, including safeguarding, so law reform is a possible outcome of the review. The issue of safeguarding is discussed in more detail in Chapter 4.

Critical practice and gerontological social work

Over the past two decades, adult social services have become increasingly characterised by bureaucratic procedures. An increased emphasis on procedural practice, along with a drift towards assessment being seen as a means of testing for eligibility, have ill served older people and professional social work practice with older people. The consequence of an increasingly bureaucratic approach to social work has, it is argued, resulted in barriers to using professional knowledge; over time, this has contributed to a loss of confidence in using professional knowledge. McDonald *et al.* (2008: 1382) argued:

> there is a real risk that staff concentrate on the minutiae of putting care services together ... hence this becomes something that anyone can do as long as they can complete the forms and professional knowledge and skills, being under-used, wither ... and staff are unable to articulate their knowledge base.

Manthorpe *et al.* (2008a), in research with older people, their carers and voluntary-sector groups, found that social workers' roles were often seen as unclear in the context of a confusing social care system that was difficult to navigate. The research highlighted the value that older people placed on social workers who were well informed, knowledgeable and practised from a person-centred perspective. Criticisms were commonplace when older people experienced social workers as being overly concerned with rationing and bureaucracy, and where their knowledge base was experienced as sparse or inadequate.

While we would argue that there has never been a 'golden age' of social work practice with older people, it does appear that successive reforms aimed at modernising social services have not always achieved the outcomes and improvements that were desired and may have contributed to a limited and proceduralised approach to practice with older people. Compelling evidence highlights that responses to the support needs of older people, especially those who have the highest or most complex support needs, have often been focused on traditional services and reductionist approaches to assessment, with an emphasis on confirming eligibility (e.g. Bowers, 2009; Blood, 2010).

Social workers need to be able to regain their professional confidence as well as more clearly to articulate and demonstrate the knowledge, skills and values that they bring to practice with older people. This is clearly vital if they are not to be accused of irrelevance or for it to be assumed that their unique contribution can be achieved by other workers (e.g. Lymbery, 2005). In a complex and changing world, social workers somehow need to be able to balance their commitments to service users and communities they seek to serve, as well as to their employing organisation and their profession (Hughes and Wearing, 2007). The review of social work roles and tasks and the subsequent Task Force report and recommendations (Department of Health, 2009c) potentially help to highlight the importance of a professional social workforce, along with the need to reaffirm and develop the professional identity of social work and promote the importance of the social work role. Critical practice highlights the importance of practitioners being able to handle uncertainty and change in the context of continuing to be able to work effectively and confidently within a professional skill, knowledge and value base (Glaister, 2010: 8).

Critical practice is underpinned by a recognition that social work practice works with situations of complexity where professional certainty can rarely be achieved and is not desirable. A forced expectation that a practitioner must 'know' the answers is likely to result in defensive and narrow practice that minimises theorising and evidence building in favour of narrow 'solutions' (e.g. Ray *et al.*, 2009; Glaister, 2010). This sort of practice might

Table 2.1 Knowledge, skills and values in critical practice

Values	Skills	Knowledge
Countering stereotypes and stigma associated with ageing	The ability to communicate complex and comprehensive information to older people with high support needs and to their families and supporters	Moving beyond a deficit perspective to enable assessments to be co-produced and include strengths and resources as well as outcomes desired by older people
Working to create conditions for empowerment, especially for older people who are perceived as being 'powerless'	Managing complex ethical dilemmas	Ability to evaluate and use gerontological research and other forms of research and knowledge
Promoting the citizenship rights and human rights of all older people, regardless of the complexity of their needs	Using creative and relevant communication strategies for people with specific communication challenges	Reflexive engagement and understanding of the impact that practice has on self and experiences of ageing
Making visible the experiences of older people	Using interpersonal skills to develop positive relationships with older people, including those identified as hard to reach or in need of statutory assessment/investigation	Understanding of and ability to confidently use legal frameworks for the benefit of older people
Working with multiple perspectives and negotiating solutions in complex systems	Responding creatively to complex situations and not being content to offer off-the-peg solutions	Able to use knowledge to theorise and weigh up evidence and circumstances as part of professional judgement and decision making
Working in difficult and complex territory, for example ethical dilemmas involving balancing rights and risk, autonomy and complex needs	Having the skill to intervene purposefully with people experiencing complex transitions or interpersonal difficulties and who are engaged in difficult decisions and choices	An understanding of a life-course perspective on ageing
	Working confidently in systems and with different agendas and perspectives	
	The ability to work confidently with risk and in undertaking risk assessment	
	Having the skill to work with people with complex needs (e.g. health conditions, end of life, people with cognitive impairment)	

be characterised by an over-focus on practical tasks, risk-averse practice and prescriptive encounters.

Glaister (2010) highlights the importance of respecting each other as equals in a critical practice context. This principle recognises that there is an imbalance of power between, for example, older people and professional workers. A commitment to making a difference and working to achieve effective and positive working relationships with older people and their families can help to uncover the meanings and subjective experiences that older people may have about their situations, which can in turn assist older people in articulating their aspirations and the outcomes for which they hope from support services.

Table 2.1 illustrates the ways in which critical gerontological practice can bring together knowledge, skills and values that are relevant to positive and creative practice with older people. Critical practice is not a 'magic bullet' and it is only part of the story. Organisations too must recognise that a changing landscape for practice involves culture change and challenging traditional assumptions about, for example, commissioning for older people. However, critical practice does surface the importance of social work offering a skilful and relevant contribution to complex and uncertain situations, as well as offering a unique contribution grounded in, for instance, social theory.

Critical practice may contribute to ensuring that professional assessments and interventions are based on a sound analysis and understanding of a person's needs and desired outcomes, rather than adopting an 'off-the-shelf' solution. This approach also means that social workers cannot be part of a landscape that assumes that older people are passive and grateful recipients of whatever care they can get.

Conclusion

This chapter has attempted to put age into context, as well as to define and address the issues of ageing within contemporary Britain. Opportunities are presented by an ageing society in which new lifestyles, careers and work locations are emerging and there is an emphasis on 'active ageing' and on intergenerational issues. It is crucial for social workers to understand this potential of ageing, as their experiences will, by definition of their role, be concentrated on frail older people and their carers, who face such problems that they are forced to seek help from formal sources. Such problems may be linked to transitions and crises such as bereavement or substance misuse.

To make sense of the situation of older people, social workers need to have knowledge of theory, research, policy and legislation, as well as the ability to reflect on their own practice. All these factors are crucial in framing social work with older people. Social workers are, however, also agents of the state and their role is defined by legislation and policy. We address both the legislative and organisational policy context under which social work operates in Chapter 3.

Putting it into practice

1 What can social workers do to contribute positively to addressing health inequalities around the experience of depression among older people?
2 Explore the literature to find out how many older people over the age of 60 have a learning disability and how many older people over 80 are carers for adult sons and daughters with a learning disability. Identify what the social work role might be in achieving outcomes for an older adult with learning disabilities who may be supported by their parents. What might the potential challenges and tensions be? How could you seek to work positively to overcome those challenges and tensions?

Further resources

Beeston, D. (2006) *Older People and Suicide*, Stoke-on-Trent: Centre for Ageing and Mental Health, Staffordshire University, http://www.staffs.ac.uk/assets/Suicide_and_older_people_tcm44-32414.pdf, accessed 7 September 2011.
A comprehensive review of the knowledge and evidence base on suicide and older age. It is also an excellent source of further information and resources.

Glaister, A. (2008) 'Introducing critical practice', in S. Fraser and S. Matthews (eds) *The Critical Practitioner in Social Work and Health Care*, London: Sage/Open University, pp 8–27.
Provides an overview of critical practice in a social work and health care context.

Ray, M., Bernard, M. and Phillips, J. (2009) *Critical Issues in Social Work with Older People*. Basingstoke: Palgrave Macmillan.
A detailed examination of the role of critical gerontological social work.

Joseph Rowntree, www.jrf.org.uk
The Joseph Rowntree Foundation is a charity that funds a large UK-wide research programme. The website has a wealth of information about the social inequalities facing older people and useful 'research round-ups' that highlight key research on a particular issue or theme.

Office of National Statistics, www.ons.gov.uk
This website has a 'focus on older people' section, which contains accessible statistical information on the lives of older people in Britain.

Stroke Association, www.stroke.org.uk
This website provides information about local support groups and services for people who have had a stroke and their supporters. The pages also have practical information about stroke and information about stroke research.

Down's Syndrome Association, www.downs-syndrome.org.uk
This website is of interest to anyone working with a person with Down's syndrome. It contains practical guidance as well as specific information about dementia and Down's syndrome. The organisation is part of the Learning Disabilities Coalition.

CHAPTER 3

The policy and organisational context of social work with older people in England

CHAPTER OVERVIEW
- Reviews developments towards the personalisation of adult care services.
- Highlights that social work takes place in a landscape characterised by change and uncertainty.
- Highlights the key principles underpinning mental capacity legislation.
- Identifies the current national eligibility criteria for access to personal social services.

Introduction

Adult welfare services have been dominated in the past two decades by care-management processes and practices underpinned by the National Health Service and Community Care Act (NHSCCA) (Department of Health, 1990). One of the key elements of the Act is the duty to offer an assessment of need for any person who may be in need of personal social services. In essence, the care management process is broken into the following:

- Screening and identifying eligibility for an assessment of need.
- Identifying the nature of assessment (e.g. simple assessment vs complex or comprehensive assessments of need); offering an assessment of need to the person providing or intending to provide informal care.
- Identifying need and determining eligibility of need.
- Prioritising needs and identifying ways to meet those needs in a care plan.
- Determining the financial contribution of a service user to the cost of those services.

• Providing the services and resources and ensuring that they are appropriately reviewed and monitored.

In 2000, it became possible for older people to access direct payments to purchase their support needs. This provision was further enhanced by the Carers and Disabled Children Act 2000, extending payments to carers. Despite local authorities being obliged to offer direct payments to any eligible person, the numbers of service users, especially older people, in receipt of direct payments has remained consistently low.

At the time of writing, current policy in England is focused on the personalisation of support and care services, with an emphasis on the development of personal budgets and direct payments (Department of Health, 2008a, 2010c). This policy has significant implications for the organisation of personal social services and the likelihood of significant culture change as well as changing roles for social workers.

The landscape of change is further reinforced by a Law Commission Review of current legislation for adult social care. One realistic possibility at the time of writing is that a single piece of legislation for access to personal social services for adults will emerge following the Law Commission's recommendations based on its review of current arrangements for adult social care (Law Commission, 2010, 2011). This need has, to a large extent, been caused by the complex and fragmented nature of adult legislation covering duties and powers to provide services and resources for adults deemed to be in need of those services. The review has also examined the possibility of developing specific duties for investigation and intervention in safeguarding adults who use adult care services. The future funding of personal social services has been on the political agenda for a considerable while and at the time of writing, recommendations made by the Dilnott Review (Commission on Funding of Care and Support, 2011) are being considered by the present government.

We begin this chapter by briefly summarising major legislation and policy since the early 1940s in the provision of welfare services for older people. We then move on to examine the aims and potential implications of the personalisation agenda and other significant legal and policy developments, namely The Mental Capacity Act, 2005 and the National Dementia Strategy, which have an impact on practice with older people.

Personal social services for older people: Overview

The primary underlying issues that have influenced successive reforms to welfare services for older people have sought to address the following:

- Deinstitutionalisation, with the growth of community care provision of a range of services responding to the needs of older disabled people.
- A concern about an ageing population and the implications for public expenditure.
- A number of scandals about the poor care of older people in residential and other forms of institutional care.
- Care *in* the community becoming care *by* the community.
- Ideological commitment by the government to develop marketised welfare services and to reduce the role of local authorities in the direct provision of services.
- Lack of clarity over which statutory agency held responsibility for what task.
- Lack of a coherent policy framework for personal social services for adults who need support.
- Inflexible and traditional services not meeting the needs of older people and their carers.
- The imperative to reduce the health and social care 'divide' and promote inter-professional and collaborative working.

Box 3.1 Policy/legislative overview, 1948–2008

- **The Beveridge Report, 1942** – Counselled against being 'lavish in old age' and recommended that pensions should be set below the subsistence level to promote thrift.
- **National Assistance Act, 1948** – Local authorities are enabled under section 29(1) to promote the welfare of older people. Section 21 of the NAA 1948 places a duty on local authorities to 'provide residential accommodation for persons who, by reason of age, illness, disability or any other circumstances, are in need of care and attention which are not otherwise available to them'. Section 47 contains the power to remove a person from their own home in specific circumstances.
- **Royal Commission on Population, 1949** – Noted the increasing population of older people and saw this as a threat to the nation's prosperity.

- **Phillips Report, 1953** – Looked at the economic and financial problems involved in providing for old age.
- **Mental Health Act, 1959** – Recommended care in the community; closure of Victorian asylums.
- **Health Services and Public Health Act, 1968** – Made arrangements for the provision of meals and recreation, visiting and social work services, adaptations, warden services and boarding out, as well as assistance in transport to services.
- **Chronically Sick and Disabled Persons Act, 1970** – Local authorities required under section 2 to assess individual need and provide services to meet the needs of disabled people.
- *A Happier Old Age*, **DHSS, 1979** – A discussion document about whether community care could keep people out of residential care, warning that 'The rise in the elderly population puts a great strain on all our pockets.'
- *Care in the Community* **Green Paper, 1981** – Considered joint financing to promote moves out of hospital.
- *Growing Older* **White Paper, 1981** – A discussion document, produced by the Conservative Government, reinforcing the idea that care in the community must increasingly mean care by the community; that is, `informal' care.
- *Care in Action* **White Paper, 1981** – Recommended strengthening neighbourhood and community support.
- **DHSS Supplementary Benefit rules change, 1981** – providing public support to residents of private and voluntary homes. This had major repercussions for the growth of private residential care.
- *The Rising Tide*, **1982** – A Hospital Advisory Service report on the prevalence of dementia.
- **Mental Health Act, 1983** – Obliged authorities within the resources available to promote community care for mentally ill people.
- *Social Services Provision of Care to the Elderly*, **1983** – DoE Audit Inspectorate found patchy and inefficient distribution of resources across the country; recommended home-care organisers as coordinators of community care.
- *Making a Reality of Community Care*, **Audit Commission, 1986** – Audit Commission again reinforced Ineffective service delivery and geographical inequality.
- **Firth Report, 1987** – Against concerns that older people were entering private residential care unnecessarily, focused on assessment of need and concluded that public support for residential care was justified.

- *From Home Help to Home Care*, **1987** – Social Services Inspectorate Report identified deficiencies in the technical efficiency of home-care services.
- **Griffiths Report, 1988** – Recommended social services to be 'enablers' rather than 'providers'.
- *Caring for People: Community Care in the Next Decade and Beyond*, **1989** – White Paper advocating a wide spectrum of services to people in their own homes, to be provided by the independent and public sectors, but acknowledging that the bulk of care is provided by family and friends.
- **NHS and Community Care Act, 1990** – Major legislation telling social services they would be the lead agency in community care; introducing the purchaser–provider split and a mixed economy of social care.
- **Community Care (Direct Payments Act), 1995**
- **Carers Recognition and Services Act, 1995**
- **Disability Discrimination Acts, 1995 and 2005**
- **Care Standards Act, 2000** – Supported by national standards for residential care, the CSA set out to identify quality standards of care for people in residential care. The Act also made provision for the protection of vulnerable people from abuse and neglect.
- **Carers and Disabled Children Act, 2000** – Provides carers with an entitlement to an assessment of needs independent to an assessment of need for the person for whom they are caring. The Act also allows direct payments to be made to carers.
- **Community Care (Delayed Discharges) Act, 2003** – Introduced charges on local authorities for hospital beds that are taken up by older people awaiting a social care service, with the aim of reducing delayed discharges from hospital beds.
- **Carers (Equal Opportunities) Act, 2005** – Amends the 1995 and 2000 Acts. Local authorities have a duty to offer an entitlement to carers of an assessment of need. Carers should be supported to continue to undertake leisure, training, work or education.
- **Mental Capacity Act, 2005** – A wide-ranging Act covering decision making; best interests; lasting power of attorney; advance decisions; and the role of the Court of Protection.
- **National Health Service Act, 2006** – Establishes a duty for local authorities to provide specific services for people experiencing mental disorder and to prevent mental disorder.

- **Mental Health Act, 2007** – Addressed a change in professional roles (for example Approved Mental Health Practitioner) and developed a new community treatment order.
- **Health and Social Care Act, 2008** – Entitlements to receive direct payments are extended to people who lack capacity.

The National Health Service and Community Care Act (NHSCCA), 1990 was primarily responsible for the organisation of personal social services into care management and community care provision. The main driver behind the NHSCCA was to curb public expenditure on residential care after the government of the day had created a 'perverse incentive' in relation to community care, allowing a subsidy for entry to private residential care through the social security budget (Phillips, 1992). The Griffiths Report (Griffiths, 1988), which led to the NHSCCA (HMSO, 1990b), also sought to address the difficulties in social work high-lighted by the Audit Commission in 1986. Through the establishment of care management, Griffiths advocated a 'needs-led' rather than a 'service-driven' approach, governed by assessment and negotiation of care packages as well as monitoring and reviewing outcomes with users and carers. Griffiths thereby identified the need for community care policy to focus on the individual user and carer for those people deemed to be most in need (that is, services would be prioritised).

Community care policy was also ideologically committed to the marketisation of welfare services and sought to decrease the role of local authorities as providers of personal social services, alongside the stimulation of services from the independent and voluntary sectors. It was anticipated that a well-developed marketplace would drive up standards through competition, thereby keeping costs competitive and enhancing choice for community care 'consumers' (i.e. service users). The degree to which the development of a market enhanced choice or empowered users of personal social services is highly questionable. Service users often did not have the opportunity to exercise choice through 'exiting' from care services and exercising choice about, for example, which provider to choose was often little more than illusory.

The modernisation agenda, personified by the Labour Government, continued a managerialist approach and extended it by giving greater emphasis to partnership, quality and continuous improvement (Waine and Henderson, 2003). The modernisation agenda was underpinned by a wish to evidence performance and accountability via target setting, benchmarking and performance indicators with reforms that sought to address:

- Decisions about care being service driven despite efforts to change commissioning approaches.
- Poor and difficult access to services, advice and information.
- Lack of participation of people who use services in influencing service-delivery developments.
- Tighter eligibility criteria providing services to fewer people.

Modernising social and health services therefore focused on developing a change agenda at central government level and driving change out from the centre to local communities. This can be seen, for example, in the National Service Framework for Older People (Department of Health, 2001b), a centrally developed policy giving strategic direction to the development of provision to older people on a number of key goals, for example developing 'person-centred' services, reducing falls and stamping out age-based discrimination. The process of managerialisation emphasised a practice environment characterised by attention to increased productivity (e.g. throughput of assessments and referrals); increased use of technology to manage workloads; developing a disciplined workforce (for example through the use of increasingly proceduralised guidance); and the role of managers in achieving appropriate levels of performance (Harris, 2008).

A critique of managerialist strategies in respect of personal social services is that the reforms have not necessarily led to a consistent level of improvement in the experience of people who use services, in practice with older people or, indeed, in the ways in which services are developed and commissioned (McDonald *et al.*, 2008). Increased time spent on the practicalities of putting together care services and the associated emphasis on IT tasks and procedures has created a drift towards bureaucratic compliance in social work practice, where assessment has been increasingly perceived as a tool to evidence eligibility for allocation of scarce resources. This has had the impact at times of moving us further away from the idea of professional assessment.

The idea of personalisation via self-directed support has its roots in the disabled people's movement, who argued that traditional community care provision emphasises an individualised (and medicalised) approach to physical and cognitive impairment. That is, community care services have focused on a disabled person's individual 'problems' or 'needs' rather than their rights as citizens (see e.g. Oliver and Sapey, 2006). Services have tended to focus on meeting 'care' needs rather than on enabling a person to make individual decisions about their support requirements and how these are achieved. Moreover, services have been provided on the basis of what is available via traditional approaches to commissioning and have often been narrow in their remit (e.g. attention to physical care needs; Renshaw, 2008). Access to self-directed support via direct payments means that (eligible) disabled people can, based on a resource allocation (how much money the local authority will allocate to meet identified outcomes), purchase and arrange support services flexibly and in a way that meets their particular requirements. In theory, such an approach will respond to a wider range of outcomes (for example, support requirements to ensure that disabled people can work, access education and make personal life-style choices) rather than simply meeting personal care needs. This also chimes with the present government's commitment to promote a devolution of responsibility from the centre to people and local communities. The principles of the personalisation agenda are defined in a Green Paper, 'A vision for social care: Capable communities and active citizens' (Department of Health, 2010a):

- *Personalisation* – increasing choice and autonomy via the use of direct payments as far as possible by 2013. This has implications for current arrangements for financial structures, assessment and commissioning services. Personalisation should involve a stronger emphasis on outcomes and give people who use services a choice as to how those outcomes are met. The Department of Health (2010a) argues that all eligible people who use services, including those people with the most complex needs, should be able to benefit from personalised services, including direct payments.
- *Prevention* – with an emphasis on communities taking responsibility for developing responsive and local community resources and services.
- *Partnership* – care and support delivered in the context of established partnerships between individual budget holders, health and social care and other agencies, such as housing.
- *Plurality* – supporting the growth of a market that responds to the support services that people want to purchase via direct payments.

- *Protection* – a belief that personalised services will result in more effective safeguarding of vulnerable adults.
- *Productivity* – agreed quality outcomes will provide a framework for expected achievements by the public sector in response to personalisation.
- *People* – a skilled workforce who can respond flexibly and creatively to the personalisation agenda.

A significant proposal within current policy focuses on moves towards self-assessment (Department of Health, 2010a) or people who are eligible for an assessment of need undertaking their own assessment. The potential benefits of self-assessment are argued on two counts. The first is that disabled people are experts in understanding their own needs and are, therefore, best placed to determine what their needs are (and how best to meet them). The second is that social work assessment has become increasingly linked to tests of eligibility and a means of gatekeeping services (e.g. Glendinning, 2008; Lymbery and Postle, 2010). This has the consequence of associating professional assessment with gatekeeping and against the spirit of personalisation which perhaps fails to recognise the complex and difficult decisions that social workers make in the context of research-constrained local authorities. The foregrounding of assessment of little more than a means of testing eligibility overlooks the benefits of professional assessment (Lymbery and Postle, 2010).

Undoubtedly, disabled people will very often have the most complete understanding of their support needs. But a person's needs may be characterised by complexity, uncertainty and change, or key people in their support system (for example informal carers) may have competing priorities. It is possible, for instance, to work with a service user with a complex and advanced condition such as multiple sclerosis whereby the person's needs change almost daily. These kinds of circumstances suggest that assessment, to be effective, must continue to be seen as a process that is revisited and not as a one-off event. Sometimes, a person may not have the capacity to demonstrate understanding of the nature of their support needs or, indeed, any risks for which they may need to have regard. Moreover, a person may not have the knowledge to make choices and decisions about the best way to meet their support needs (see e.g. Priestley, 2004; Renshaw, 2008). It seems likely, therefore, that a significant number of people may require support or assistance to express their needs and without it may make decisions that do not serve their interests.

Accessing direct payments for personal assistance means that individual service users will, in effect, become employers of their own care/support team. This is argued to involve a number of direct contrasts to the often-cited inflexibility of services brokered by social services. Leece (2010) has suggested that employing personal assistants can create opportunities to:

- Choose workers and shape the relationship between employer and personal assistant.
- Determine the boundaries of the relationship.
- Be more reciprocal and set the the agenda.
- Have some power and autonomy in setting terms and conditions.
- Ensure that individual interests and aspirations have precedence or are given appropriate attention.

However, Leece (2010) has also reported the potential vulnerability of personal assistants who become close to a person and, as a result, work longer than they are paid to do. Employing personal assistants requires service users to move from citizens as consumers to citizens as managers and entrepreneurs, as well as managers of public funds (Scourfield, 2007: 116). While this may provide opportunities for disabled people to manage their own support requirements, not everyone will want or feel able to engage with this level of personal budget management. The orientation towards personal budgets as a means of enabling people to, for example, return to work, while an appropriate aim for some, does little to reflect an understanding of the diversity of need that older people may experience as a result of cognitive impairment, stroke, falls or limiting illness (Lloyd, 2010). Understanding that older people may not want to manage a personal budget is 'not the same as denying their right to be fully engaged in decisions affecting their care – rather, it is a practical response to people's lived reality' (Lymbery and Postle, 2010: 2515).

These issues have a clear implication for social work practice. It seems critical to gerontological social work that practitioners ensure that older people with the most complex needs, who have also been vulnerable to marginalisation and access to poor or unequal services, are not further discriminated against because they do not access a direct payment. This raises ethical questions too (Lloyd, 2010), in terms of ensuring that people with the most complex needs are treated well, as well as serving as a reminder that public-sector services emerged to support people who were 'necessarily dependent' and ensure that they 'are treated with respect and dignity, to ensure a collectivised approach to risk, and to ensure that secure and reliable forms of support outside the market and family are available' (Scourfield, 2007: 108).

The opportunities that access to personal budgets and direct payments could bring to people who use services may be considerable. A lack of choice and flexibility in the way needs are responded to has been a criticism of many formal services. We must take seriously any development that enhances the likelihood of people being able genuinely to exercise choice and freedom about how their needs are met. Alongside the potential benefits that may accrue to people who need support, there are a number of issues that have to be clarified and properly aired, however.

Fair Access to Care and eligibility criteria

The 1990s were characterised by increasing targeting of services to those people in greatest need. However, a lack of consistency between local councils in their provision of services to people with similar needs led to the government introducing national eligibility criteria, Fair Access to Care or FACs (Department of Health, 2003). Four bands describing differing levels of risk were constructed: critical, substantial, moderate and low (Department of Health, 2003).

In 2010, new guidance on the eligibility criteria (Department of Health, 2010c) was introduced under section 7(1) of the Local Authority Social Services Act 1970. The guidance takes account of personalisation, including information about developing preventative services. It also considers what local authorities should do in response to people who are deemed ineligible for support services, as well as the importance of early recognition of those who might experience particular risk.

Critically, the guidance does not propose a hierarchy of need unless that need is of a life-threatening nature, or there are significant safeguarding issues. Thus, it is argued that needs relating to social participation or inclusion should be seen as just as important as personal care needs:

a disabled person who is facing significant obstacles in taking up education and training to support their independence and well-being should be given equal weight to an older person who is unable to perform vital personal care tasks – and vice versa. Councils should make decisions within the context of a human rights approach. (Department of Health, 2010c)

It is recognised that local authorities are unlikely to be able to make large investments in prevention, but the guidance, together with the Green Paper on social care (Department of Health, 2010a), highlight government expectation of an investment in health and health promotion; this leads to a potentially significant role for social workers if local authorities become the lead agency in addressing health inequalities (Department of Health, 2010c). The guidance also requires local authorities to provide advice and information for people who do not meet the eligibility threshold for service provision. This might include assisting a person to complete a support plan and signposting them to other services to resource the plan; improved benefits take-up and other advice and information are also suggested as important areas of input for people who are ineligible within eligibility criteria. How this would work out in practice is not clear, nevertheless.

Mental capacity

Gerontological social workers will be particularly concerned about the principles and practice underpinned by the Mental Capacity Act, 2005, as it provides a crucial legislative framework to help in the consideration of whether a person has the decision making capacity to take specific decisions. The legislation covers three main areas:

- Part One: lasting power of attorney, advance decisions, Independent Mental Capacity Advocate.
- Part two: Court of Protection and Public Guardian.
- Part three: general provisions (Brammer, 2010: 479).

The Act is underpinned by five principles:

- A person must be assumed to have capacity unless it is established that s/he does not.
- All practicable steps must be taken to assist a person to demonstrate their ability to make a decision.
- Unwise or foolhardy decisions should not be construed as a person lacking capacity.

- Any decision or act made on behalf of a person who lacks capacity must be done so on the basis of the person's best interests.
- Any decision or act made on behalf of a person who lacks capacity must be made on the basis of it being the least restrictive option available.

The principle of assumed capacity is very important, as it highlights that it is *not* acceptable, for example, to assume that an older person lacks capacity because they have a diagnosis of dementia. Similarly, it offers a critical guide to practice as capacity is decision specific. This means, for example, that if someone lacks capacity to make decisions in one area (such as managing finance), it should not be assumed or implied that they lack capacity in another area of their life.

Practice focus

Lasting power of attorney

Mr Jones has fairly recently been diagnosed with Alzheimer's disease and lives on his own in his family home. He was widowed several years ago. Mr Jones is in generally good health and enjoys being outdoors in the garden. He keeps some chickens and has always grown vegetables. His son, who lives locally, has taken him to the shops each week for groceries. On the whole, he manages his day-to-day life pretty well and has kept a similar routine for many years, which helps him to organise his week.

Lately, Mr Jones has struggled to pay his bills and finds it difficult to recall if he has had his pension and whether he owes any money. This has become a source of great worry to him. In discussion with his son, Mr Jones was fully able to appreciate the stress of worrying about his finances. He agreed to nominate a lasting power of attorney and was judged to have capacity to make this decision because he could:

- Understand what a lasting power of attorney could do if, in the future, he lost capacity to make decisions about aspects of his personal welfare.
- Retain this information by referring to a memory board about what a lasting power of attorney might do to support him.
- Identify that he wanted his son to take on the role of lasting power of attorney and communicate this decision to his solicitor.

Brammer (2010) makes the point that an assessment of capacity will often be carried out on a day-to-day basis by people who are in close contact, for example support workers, relatives. However,

> Professional involvement may be required for an assessment of capacity in some circumstances, including more complex decisions ... where the decision has serious consequences; a person challenges the finding that he lacks capacity; family members, carers and/or professionals disagree about a person's capacity; the person being assessed is expressing different views to different people; somebody has been accused of abusing a vulnerable adult who may lack capacity to make decisions to protect them; and a person repeatedly makes decisions that puts them at risk. (Brammer, 2010: 483)

This guidance means, for example, that an older person may not be moved to a care home simply because care at home is inadequate, or a family member thinks that the person will be 'better off' in a care home. If there are concerns that someone lacks capacity to make a decision about where they should live or the sort of support they might need, then an assessment of mental capacity would focus on that area of decision making, rather than making any global statements about their 'capacity'. The Act makes it clear that assessment should make every effort to:

- Ensure that the person can communicate capacity (for example, finding accessible ways to communicate).
- Make sure that the person has access to treatment if it is having an impact on their decision making capacity (for example, they may lack mental capacity on a temporary basis because they have delirium caused by infection).
- Devising an intervention to help the person make particular decisions (for example use of a calendar, Talking Mats, learning new skills via rehabilitation).
- Assessment should also take place at different times or locations (for example, a person with dementia may find it harder to engage and understand in the morning but much easier in the afternoon; sometimes people may have conditions that fluctuate and this should be taken account of, for example by asking the question: 'Is this a decision that must be taken now, or can we wait and see if the person's decision making capacity about this issue improves?'

Box 3.2 What are best interests?

If a person is judged to lack decision making capacity about a specific issue, decisions made on their behalf must be made on the basis of their 'best interests' – and must have regard for (Brammer, 2010: 484):

- What their best interests are.
- Their past and present wishes (if known).
- Beliefs and values likely to influence their decision.
- Other factors they might consider relevant.
- The views of other people who are appropriate to consult.

Any decisions made on the basis of best interests must be carefully recorded, giving clear information about:

- How the decision was reached.
- Who was consulted about it.
- What factors were taking into account when making the decision.

Practice focus

Best interests

Mrs Harding has lived in the Summerville Nursing Home in Worcestershire for two years. She was judged to be well settled in the home and was receiving funding support via the local authority. Mrs Harding has multi-infarct dementia following a series of smaller strokes and also a significant stroke three years ago. She came to live in the nursing home following the death of her husband, as it was located close to her family home of 40 years and local church. Her daughter, who lives in Scotland, decided that she wanted Mrs Harding to move to a nursing home in Scotland so that she could see more of her. The nursing home manager contacted the local authority to express her concern about this decision as Mrs Harding, in her view, did not have capacity to make the decision and he daughter was not identified as having a lasting power of attorney. Mrs Harding had no other relatives.

A social worker reviewed Mrs Harding's support at the nursing home as well as assessing her decision making capacity about where she lived. The assessment determined that she was not able to understand information relevant to making a decision about moving to another area or another home, nor was she able to retain the necessary information in order to weigh up the possibility of moving against staying where she was. In the assessment, a number of communication tools were used (photographs, Talking Mat, spoken word, observation of wellbeing and how Mrs Harding responded to life in the nursing home). The social worker judged that Mrs Harding did not have the decision making capacity to make a judgement about moving to Scotland. She also made a referral to an Independent Mental Capacity Advocate to provide independent representation and support to Mrs Harding in respect of an assessment of her decision making capacity and any subsequent actions that were taken.

The Independent Mental Capacity Advocate also took the view that Mrs Harding was not able to make a decision about moving to Scotland and that it was in her best interests to remain in the nursing home. In making this decision, the following factors were ascertained:

- Mrs Harding had participated in decisions about moving to the nursing home two years ago following the death of her husband.
- The nursing home was run by a Catholic Trust and Mrs Harding had been a practising Catholic all her life.
- Mrs Harding's records and interviews with the nursing home manager and other staff indicated that she was settled and well cared for. There was no discernible evidence that she had indicated any desire to live closer to her daughter and no evidence was obtained that she was able to understand the implications of her daughter living in Scotland.

However, Mrs Harding recognised her daughter from photographs and DVDs and was always thrilled to see her. She was visibly distressed and anxious when her daughter left after a visit. It was felt on balance that this was a 'normal' reaction to being separated and did not constitute sufficient information to warrant removing her to Scotland.

Mrs Harding's daughter refused to accept that a move to Scotland was not in her mother's best interest and so the matter was referred to the Court of Protection for their jurisdiction.

Social work with older people will involve full and appropriate use of the Mental Capacity Act legislation. This may also include, for example, being aware of any advance decisions that a service user may have made about future medical treatment, as well as any identified lasting power of attorney that is in place. Indeed, older people may need help to access advice and information about these aspects of the mental capacity legislation and may wish to discuss them with a practitioner. Social workers may also be involved with the Court of Protection. This is responsible for determining issues of capacity on specific matters as well as resolving disputes about capacity (Brammer, 2010).

National Dementia Strategy

People living with dementia have been an under-recognised group in policy, service development and practice. The 'Forget-me-Not' report (Audit Commission, 2000) highlighted a history of fragmented and poorly developed services for older people with dementia (and older people with other mental health problems). There is considerable evidence of age-based discrimination in formal services and poor standards of care for older people remain an issue of concern (Parliamentary and Health Service Ombudsman, 2011). For older people with dementia, negative attitudes about ageing, coupled with stigma and stereotypes associated with dementia, may result in a 'double jeopardy' of discrimination (Morris and Morris, 2010).

The National Dementia Strategy (Department of Health, 2009b) was the first national strategy for the development of a comprehensive policy aimed at addressing some the inadequacies of dementia care and creating an overall improvement in the experience of people living with dementia. The Strategy focused on a number of key areas for improvement:

- Raising awareness and understanding of dementia.
- Early diagnosis and support.
- Improving the quality of life for people living with dementia.
- Improving the ability of the workforce to work positively with people living with dementia.

The National Dementia Strategy was reviewed and updated (Department of Health, 2010b) to focus on four national priorities:

- Good-quality early diagnosis and intervention.
- Improved quality of care for people with dementia in hospital.
- Improved quality of life for people living with dementia in care homes.
- Reduced use of anti-psychotic medication.

Social workers will undoubtedly have a role to play in shaping positive practice for people living with dementia. For example, ensuring that the person has a high-quality assessment of need, including an understanding of their biography, can help to shape an individualised plan. This is vital in, for example, highlighting the support needs and preferences if the person moves to a care home or other form of supported housing. Social workers may also play an important role in helping an older person refer themselves to primary health care for investigation of memory problems or other forms of cognitive difficulty. There is a need to encourage creative development of support services for people living with dementia. Social work practitioners may play a crucial role in identifying areas of need in communities and working with people living with dementia to encourage their participation in service development and commissioning. Crucially, social work practitioners should work to ensure, via their particular skill and knowledge base, that people with dementia are not discriminated against on the basis of their age or cognitive abilities and that they are able to receive good-quality support services.

Conclusion

This chapter has discussed and highlighted aspects of the complex and changing policy landscape in adult social care. The personalisation agenda, with its emphasis on self-directed care and direct payments, will doubtless continue to have a profound impact on the way in which social work and the wider health and social care workforce are organised. It is important that social workers are able to articulate their role and contribution to the personalisation agenda as well as to ask questions about the proposed changes.

As we have argued in the chapter, there are critical issues for older people with high support needs or who are at the end of their lives that must be addressed. It is also important that we are aware that social policy in respect of adult social care is becoming increasingly divergent across the countries of the British Isles. This again will have implications for the ways in which the social work role develops in response to these different approaches. Finally, we examined a key policy in respect of people living with dementia, a condition which, given its prevalence among older people and its importance over the coming years, will undoubtedly have a major impact on social work practice with older people.

Putting it into practice

1 In what ways can you use your social work skills to enable a
  person to demonstrate their capacity to make a decision?
2 How can social workers contribute to the development of
  preventative services and community resources?

Further resources

Brammer, A. (2010) *Social Work Law*, Harlow: Pearson Education.
  A comprehensive book detailing the legislative framework for adult
  welfare and the role of the law in social work practice.

Department of Health (2010) *A Vision for Adult Care: Capable
  Communities and Active Citizens*, London: Department of Health,
  www.dh.gov.uk.
  Green paper setting out the government's aspirations for the
  development of adult social care.

Lymbery, M. and Postle, K. (2010) 'Social work in the context of adult
  social care in England and the resultant implications for social work
  education', *British Journal of Social Work*, 40: 2502–22.
  Critical commentary on the implications of the personalisation
  agenda on social work.

Department of Health, www.dh.gov.uk.
  This website contains all of the relevant policy on adult social and
  health care.

CHAPTER 4

Safeguarding

CHAPTER OVERVIEW
- At the time of writing, there is no specific legislation in England, Wales and Northern Ireland to address the issue of adult safeguarding.
- The Law Commission has made recommendations that would clarify the duty to investigate possible abuse.
- Concern has been expressed about the particular safeguarding issues that may arise in the context of personalisation.
- Proponents of personalisation argue that self-directed support enhances the potential to work positively and openly with the risks a person might be experiencing.
- It is argued that safeguarding practice should develop within the context of personalisation rather than as a separate strand.

Introduction

There is no specific legislation in England, Wales and Northern Ireland that deals with the matter of adult safeguarding. Instead, practitioners use a wide range of statutes that are generally perceived as fragmented and disjointed (Law Commission, 2011). In contrast, Scotland has established a clear legal framework as a basis for adult safeguarding and protection (The Adult Support and Protection (Scotland) Act, 2007). Following a succession of critical commentaries, a Law Commission review was convened to make recommendations about adult safeguarding, as part of a comprehensive review of the wider landscape of adult social care statutory arrangements.

It is not possible to cover the complexity of adult safeguarding practice, policy and law in a single chapter and so we introduce the key policies relevant to safeguarding. The chapter also highlights possible law reform in adult safeguarding. Skills in working with people who often have complex support needs in a safeguarding context are considered, along with the importance of effective and accurate recording skills. The development of the personalisation agenda and specifically the issue of direct payments are discussed in relation to safeguarding issues.

Protecting or safeguarding?

The investigation of and intervention in the alleged abuse of people who are, or appear to be, eligible for community care services have typically been defined as the 'protection' of 'vulnerable adults'. Adult service users are deemed to be vulnerable by virtue of a physical or cognitive impairment, or other circumstances that may put them at particular risk of abuse and render them unable to protect themselves from harm. Dictionary definitions of the term 'vulnerable' include:

- Defenceless
- Helpless
- Susceptible
- Weak

The term 'vulnerable' carries with it powerful messages and has become the subject of concern, as it runs the risk of locating the cause of abuse with the victim and their 'vulnerability' rather than the actions of the perpetrators of the abuse. It also implies that vulnerability is an inherent characteristic of a person who uses services (e.g. ADSS, 2005: 5; Law Commission, 2010) and resonates with Fook's (2002: 13) claim that we often think of people in binary opposites (that is, dependent or independent; at risk or free from risk; vulnerable or invincible). Of course, in reality people are rarely wholly dependent, or at risk in every aspect of their lives. Critically, too, we have to ask questions about the ways in which such terms are constructed: a person deemed to be 'vulnerable' may be assumed to have some inherent and personal characteristics that make them vulnerable, whereas a state of vulnerability may be created by extrinsic factors over which they have very little control. An older person may be described as 'vulnerable to self-neglect', but if they are living in poverty, with inadequate housing and poor or sparse support networks, then their vulnerability is as much if not more about structural inequalities and the sharpening of those inequalities in older age, than it is about them being personally 'vulnerable'.

In response to these concerns, the Law Commission (2011) recommended that the term 'vulnerable' adult is replaced by adult 'at risk' of abuse. However, at the time of writing no decision has been made and consultation by the Law Commission has raised some concerns that the term 'adult at risk' is overly inclusive, as well as failing to recognise that risk is part of life and, indeed, often adds to quality of life.

The term 'safeguarding' offers a much wider definition than the notion of 'protection'. NDSS (2005) highlights that 'safeguarding' embraces both preventative and positive practice and implies a wider range of activities in support people at risk of abuse, for example:

- Reducing the likelihood of repeat episodes of abuse.
- Empowering people to safeguard themselves.
- Improving service and systems quality.
- Earlier detection of abuse.
- Analysis of safeguarding data to understand and mitigate risk factors (Rees and Manthorpe, 2010).

Safeguarding has been more fully defined as:

> a range of activity aimed at upholding an adult's fundamental right to be safe at the same time as respecting people's rights to make choices. Safeguarding involves empowerment, protection and justice ... In practice the term 'safeguarding' is used to mean both specialist services where harm or abuse has, or is suspected to have, occurred and other activity designed to promote the wellbeing and safeguard the rights of adults. (Improvement and Development Agency, 2010: 4)

This definition highlights the importance of safeguarding as an approach to all aspects of adult social care delivery, relating as it does to the broader notion of a service user's right to fair and equal treatment, to be treated with dignity and for individual rights to be preserved. Moreover, it highlights the role of proactive and preventative work as a foundation for safeguarding.

What is abuse?

Abuse is defined in *No Secrets* (Department of Health, 2000: 2.5) as:

a violation of an individual's human and civil rights by any other person or persons.

Abuse can occur in any relationship and may result in significant harm to, or exploitation of, the person subjected to it (Department of Health, 2000: 2.6). Abuse may be experienced in a number of ways:

- Single or repeated acts.
- Physical, verbal or psychological abuse.
- Act of neglect or omission to act.
- Financial or sexual transactions to which a person has not consented or cannot consent.
- Discriminatory abuse and forms of abuse such as physical abuse that are fuelled by discrimination, such as racism, sexism, homophobia.

However, more recently it has been argued that a list-type approach to defining forms of abuse has reached the end of its usefulness, given the overlapping nature of abuse. Rather, abuse often has 'no one cause or precipitating factor and needs to be analysed from a number of vantage points. Because it varies so much, there is a wide range of agencies and systems that need to be engaged on behalf of people at risk' (Brown, 2009: 308).

Practice focus

A single form of abuse?

Maisie Williams lives alone in a small rented flat. She is registered as a blind person and is no longer able to get out and about very much on her own. Her son, who lives in the town, visits her each week to collect her pension, pay her bills and do her shopping. A referral has been made by the accommodation warden because she is becoming increasingly concerned that Maisie is being financially abused by her son.

Investigation by a social worker confirms that Maisie appears to have almost no independent access to her finances, as her son 'manages' them. Maisie has very little food in the house and evidence suggests that she has lost weight over the past few months. Her flat appears cold and bare. The warden has indicated that many of Maisie's possessions (such as ornaments) have mysteriously 'disappeared' over the past few months. Maisie has received reminders for bills that she believes her son has paid or should have paid and is very worried about them. She is not sleeping well and has become anxious, tearful and afraid.

Maisie is very anxious not to offend her son, but also appears afraid of him and alludes to him having problems and not being in work. She told the social worker that when she asked for money to buy groceries during the week, a huge row ensued and her son was verbally aggressive. He called her ungrateful and threatened to withdraw his support. Maisie is afraid that if this happens, she will have no one to help her with her day-to-day needs.

Based on the information we have, Maisie may be experiencing financial abuse, as the whereabouts of her money cannot be accounted for and it is clear that she has not given consent to money being spent elsewhere. However, it is also likely that being denied access to her finances creates emotional and psychological consequences as well as a physical impact on her health (e.g. weight loss, possible risk of hypothermia and lack of access to personal comforts). It is possible that the abuse took place on the basis of opportunity (her son has access to money and valuables). However, it is likely that other, inter-related factors are relevant. Abuse may be influenced by long-term family dynamics. It is possible, for example, that domestic abuse has been part of the family history. Situational factors, such as alcohol or substance misuse, may provide a pressing motivation to access the financial means to support such misuse (Scragg and Mantell, 2008). Neglect may also be an issue, as neglect can occur intentionally or unintentionally and include failure to provide appropriate care, attention and support.

- What actions do you think could be taken to safeguard Maisie from abuse?

The prevalence of abuse

A national survey has been conducted examining the prevalence of abuse. It proposes a prevalence figure of 4 per cent (including mistreatment by neighbours and acquaintances), which equates to just under 350 000 older people being abused each year (O'Keefe *et al.*, 2007). The survey did not include older men and women living in care homes. At present, there is no equivalent study examining the prevalence of abuse of adults other than older people. However, the figures highlight the likelihood of social workers encountering older people who, for whatever reason, are at risk of potential abuse or who have actually experienced abuse. It is clearly everybody's business and something to which practitioners must be alert when they work with older people.

Messages from research

UK study of abuse and neglect (O'Keefe *et al.*, 2007)

This national prevalence survey was commissioned by Comic Relief and the Department of Health and surveyed 2111 older people living in private households in the four countries of Great Britain.

A summary of findings from the survey includes:

- 2.6 per cent of people aged 66 and over reported that they had experienced mistreatment that involved a family member, close friend or care worker during the year previous to the survey.
- When the data includes mistreatment by neighbours and acquaintances, the overall prevalence increases to 4 per cent. This equates to a figure of approximately 342 400 older people being subject some form of mistreatment each year.
- Prevalence rates for individual types of mistreatment were: neglect 1.1 per cent (11 people in 1000); financial abuse 0.7 per cent (7 people in 1000); psychological 0.4 per cent (4 people in 1000); physical 0.4 per cent (4 people in 1000); and sexual 0.2 per cent (2 people in 1000). 6 per cent of those people who had experienced mistreatment in the year prior to the survey reported two different types of mistreatment.
- 51 per cent of mistreatment involved a partner or spouse, 49 per cent another family member, 13 per cent a care worker and 5 per cent a close friend.
- 53 per cent of perpetrators of abuse were living in the respondent's house at the time of the abuse.
- Three-quarters of the research participants who had reported mistreatment indicated that the impact was either serious (43 per cent) or very serious (33 per cent). The research reported that the most commonly reported effects were emotional and social (for example, being isolated from family and friends).

Current policy and legal framework

No Secrets (Department of Health, 2000) is statutory guidance issued under section 7 of the Local Authority Social Service Act, 1970, which sets out the principles and guidelines for developing policies and procedures to protect adults from abuse (the Welsh equivalent document is entitled *In Safe Hands*). The guidance highlights important principles such as the need for organised and comprehensive inter-professional working (at all levels, from operational staff to elected members and chief officer/executive). *No Secrets* also confirmed the role of the local authority as the lead agency in developing preventative and responsive strategies, policies and procedures in responding to adult abuse.

Subsequently, the Association of Directors of Adult Social Services (ADASS, 2005) developed a framework for good-practice standards in adult protection. The document moved away from definitions of 'vulnerable' adults in need of protection, to safeguarding adults at critical levels of risk (serious abuse of neglect has occurred or will occur) and substantial levels of risk (abuse or neglect has occurred or will occur). The report sets out good-practice standards that address accessing help, responding to abuse and the importance of partnership working. Similar to *No Secrets*, it is underpinned by a focus on human rights evidenced by wellbeing, choice and independence for people who may be eligible for community care services and the importance of being able to live a life free from abuse and neglect (ADASS, 2005).

Box 4.1 Safeguarding adults

A summary of standards in *Safeguarding Adults: A National Framework of Standards for Good Practice and Outcomes in Adult Protection Work* (ADASS, 2005):

- Established multi-agency partnerships to lead on safeguarding adults work in each local authority.
- Accountability and ownership of safeguarding are recognised in each partnership organisation's executive body.
- Active promotion of the message that every person has the right to live a life free from abuse and neglect by safeguarding partnership organisations.
- Well-publicised policy of 'zero tolerance' of abuse within the organisation.
- Workforce development and training strategy in place that embraces multi-agency working and is appropriately resourced.
- All citizens can easily access information about how to gain safety from abuse and what to do to get help.
- Policies and procedures are in place to provide a framework for responding to adults who are or may be eligible for community care services and who are or may be at risk of abuse or neglect.

- Partner agencies have internal guidelines consistent with safeguarding adults policies and procedures.
- Multi-agency procedures detail the stages of activity in safeguarding (see below).
- Safeguarding procedures are written or produced in an accessible format for adults covered in the procedures.
- Partnership includes service users and has a commitment to promoting service user participation in its membership, training, monitoring, development and implementation of safeguarding strategy, policies and procedures.

In 2009, the Department of Health reviewed *No Secrets* and consulted extensively with over 12 000 participants, including 3000 citizens to whom the guidance was relevant and 9000 professionals working in the field and representing major user and special interest groups. Key messages from the consultation process with citizens included:

- The importance of empowerment as a fundamental building block of safeguarding.
- Safeguarding decisions should be taken by the individual concerned, who should be supported to retain control and make their own choices.
- Safeguarding adults is not the same as safeguarding children.
- The recognition and participation of people who lack capacity are important (Department of Health, 2009a).

There was strong support in the *No Secrets* consultation for the development of safeguarding legislation that participants felt would make safeguarding a priority and provide an unambiguous legislative basis for safeguarding activities. Participants who were opposed to specific legislation have argued the following:

- Improvements in policy and practice had been made without legislation and would continue to develop.
- Legislation would not necessarily mean that safeguarding became a priority.
- It would extend government power over individuals in an unhelpful way.
- Safeguarding should be part of mainstream activity and incorporated into the 'choice' agenda (Department of Health, 2009a: 7).

There is of course a range of existing legislation that is relevant and must be used to underpin the current arrangements for safeguarding. Brammer (2010) has suggested that the Human Rights Act (1998) may help to strengthen the *No Secrets* guidance, given its commitment to human and civil rights. Human rights articles of significance to safeguarding could include:

- Article 2 – the right to life.
- Article 3 – the right to freedom from torture and degrading treatment.
- Article 5 – the right to liberty.
- Article 8 – the right to respect for privacy and a family life.
- Article 14 – the right not to be discriminated against.

Box 4.2 summarises a range of legislation that is relevant for social workers in their safeguarding practice.

Box 4.2 Legislation relevant to safeguarding

Family Law Act, 1996

- Injunctions to prevent abuse may be applied for within this Act in respect of domestic violence.

Public Interest Disclosure Act, 1998

- Protection of workers who 'whistle blow' in good faith and in the public interest.

Criminal Justice Act, 2003

- Provisions for criminal justice and dealing with offenders.
- Places a duty on courts to increase sentences for offences found to be caused by hostility based on a victim's disability (Brammer, 2010: 519).

Sexual Offences Act, 2003

- Covers a range of sexual offences as well as defining consent to sexual activity and sexual offences with regard to people who cannot consent to sexual activity.

Domestic Violence, Crime and Victims Act, 2004

- Includes the criminal offence of death of a child or vulnerable adult (familial homicide).

Mental Capacity Act, 2005

- Assessment of mental capacity to make specific decisions and mental capacity is assumed unless demonstrated otherwise.
- The principle of best interests.
- Lasting power of attorney (appointing a person to deal with finances, health and welfare decisions if a person loses mental capacity to make decisions in those areas of their life).
- Advance decisions.
- The Court of Protection (jurisdiction to make decisions for adults who lack capacity and who do not have a lasting power of attorney in place).
- Independent Mental Capacity Advocate.
- Deprivation of liberty safeguards.
- Criminal offence (ill-treatment or wilful neglect of a person who lacks capacity).

Safeguarding Vulnerable Groups Act, 2006

- Vetting and barring scheme (to prevent unsuitable people working in health and social care).

Health and Social Care Act, 2008

- Single regulatory body for health and social care with responsibilities for the registration, inspection and regulation of regulated services (Care Quality Commission).
- A major responsibility for promoting the welfare of people who use regulated services.

Other legal provisions

- National Assistance Act, 1948 (provision of support services).
- Anti-discrimination legislation.
- Mental Health Act, 1983 (for example after-care support, guardianship).
- National Health Service and Community Care Act, 1990.

Adapted from Brammer (2010).

Investigating possible abuse

At the time of writing, the duty to assess a person is dealt with by the National Health Service and Community Care Act, 1990 (s. 47) and the *No Secrets* (Department of Health, 2000) statutory guidance in relation to investigation and intervention in adult abuse.

Box 4.3 The Law Commission review of adult social care

The Law Commission undertook a comprehensive review of current legislative provision for adult social care. This was a wide-ranging review and included current provision in respect of adult safeguarding. The Law Commission has proposed that legislation should be changed to include the following:

- A single adult social care statute that would establish a duty to investigate and take appropriate action in adult abuse.
- Clarification of the duties and powers of local authorities (as the lead co-ordinating agency) to safeguard adults from abuse and neglect.

The duty to investigate would apply to an adult at risk (defined by the person having or appearing to have social care needs; the person must be at risk of harm, must appear to be unable to safeguard themselves, and the local authority must believe that it is necessary to make enquiries).

'Harm' in the review is defined as:

- The impairment of health (physical or mental) or development (physical, intellectual, emotional, social or behavioural).
- Self-harm and neglect.
- Unlawful conduct (for example financial abuse).

Adapted from *Adult Social Care* (Law Commission, 2011), http://www.justice.gov.uk/lawcommission/docs/lc326_adult_social_care.pdf, accessed 8 September 2011.

Working together

The *No Secrets* (Department of Health, 2000) guidance highlighted the importance of cooperation and collaborative working between agencies that are involved in safeguarding at all levels. This is further reinforced by the *National Framework of Standards for Good Practice and Outcomes in Adult Protection* (ADASS, 2005). At a strategic level, *No Secrets* suggested that each local authority should develop adult Safeguarding Boards. These boards are multi-agency partnerships and should involve a wide range of statutory and voluntary-sector agencies that are involved with safeguarding adults. Safeguarding Boards are important bodies as they are responsible for:

- Facilitating and promoting joint working in adult protection and safeguarding.
- Ensuring the development of multi-agency policy and that relevant procedures are in place.
- Promoting the importance of safeguarding at all levels.
- Providing training and information.
- Conducting serious case reviews (Department of Health, 2000).

At the time of writing, adult Safeguarding Boards are not provided for in statute law. The Law Commission Review (2011) has recommended that the Boards are placed on a statutory footing and that their role and tasks should be clearly specified. It has also been proposed that adult Safeguarding Boards should be required to monitor levels of abuse as well as assess any particular trends in safeguarding and to use that research to develop preventative and timely responses to safeguarding policy and practice.

At an operational or practice level, the *No Secrets* guidance makes it clear that operational staff are responsible for identifying, investigating and responding to potential or actual abuse. Clearly, a collaborative approach to safeguarding means that practitioners across health and social care, as well as other sectors such as housing, the police, other statutory agencies and voluntary- and independent-sector agencies, need to have a common understanding of the definitions of abuse, as well as of the importance of safeguarding. The guidance also highlights the importance of a shared understanding of assessment and investigation and joint arrangements for decision making.

Point for reflection

- Refer to adult safeguarding policies and procedures in your practice learning agency or workplace.
- What is in place to encourage and promote collaborative working?
- Discuss the benefits and challenges of interagency collaborative working in safeguarding with a social work colleague.
- What specific contribution does social work make to safeguarding practice? How does this differ from other professional roles involved in safeguarding?

No Secrets guidance highlights the importance of shared principles to guide the work that organisations do collaboratively to safeguard adults:

- Actively work together within an agreed inter-agency framework.
- Promote the empowerment of and wellbeing of adults through the services they provide.
- Act in a way that supports the right of people to lead an independent life.
- Protect people who are unable to take their own decisions.
- Recognise that the right to self-determination can involve risk – this should include an open discussion between the individual and the agencies about the risk involved to that individual.
- Ensure the safety of vulnerable adults.
- Ensure that individuals receive appropriate help and support (Department of Health, 2000: 4.3).

Point for reflection

- Returning to the case study about Maisie on page 76, in what ways should the principles of good practice inform any assessment or investigation of possible abuse and intervention that you undertake with Maisie?
- What possible tensions could there be between Maisie's right to autonomy and independence and the duty to ensure the safety of vulnerable adults?

There will always be tensions between working to promote and ensure a person's right to autonomy and agency on the one hand, and the duty to provide appropriate protection to a vulnerable adult on the other. However, it is important that every effort is made so that interventions are appropriate to the level of need (that is, not paternalistic, controlling or censorious); that as far as possible interventions enable people to continue with or develop their preferred lifestyle and associated roles and activities; and that a person who has experienced abuse is not made to feel more of a victim by the way they are treated or responded to.

In Maisie's situation, it might be important to work with her to find a way to ensure that she has independent access to her finances. If Maisie has the capacity to make decisions about her finances (and there is no reason to suggest that she does not), she may insist that she wants her son to continue to manage her money, as she is worried that a change of role would spoil their relationship. In this situation it is appropriate to work with Maisie to develop a safeguarding plan. Possible strategies could be:

- Work with Maisie and her son to set up direct debit payments for rent and bills and encourage Maisie to tell her son that she needs access to her own finances.
- Offer a carer's assessment for Maisie's son, which might enable him to identify what is, or appears to be, going wrong with his management of Maisie's finances and her general situation.
- Help Maisie to find a way to do her own shopping or organise some other support to help her to shop each week.
- Negotiate with Maisie for the accommodation warden to be a point of regular contact and monitoring.
- Encourage Maisie to have her weight and health checked.
- Encourage Maisie to be more assertive in saying what she needs.

Investigation process

As we have seen, local authorities take the lead role in safeguarding and the investigation of possible abuse, but collaboration across agencies is essential. The process for investigation is outlined in Figure 4.1. Effective social work practice encompassing the knowledge, skills and values outlined in this book is fundamental to effective safeguarding practice, alongside the need to develop specialist knowledge and skills via ongoing professional development, practice experience and appropriate supervision.

Communication skills

We further highlight the importance of effective communication skills in social work with older people and describe some of the factors that may have an impact on communication styles and needs in Chapter 5. Our discussion there is located in the context of challenging the ways in which professional power can reinforce power imbalances in communication, as well as leave unchallenged assumptions about what older people 'can' and 'cannot' do. In safeguarding practice specifically, we have to guard against assumptions that older people, especially those with high support needs, will be unable to communicate effectively.

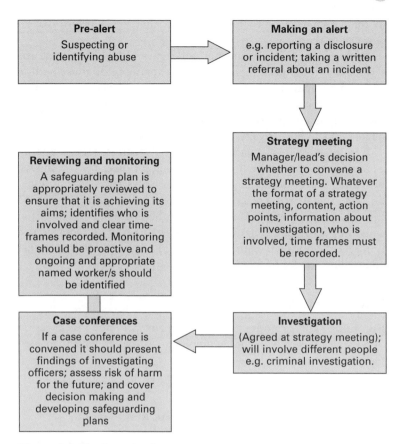

Figure 4.1 The investigation process

Alongside the ability to utilise different approaches to communication and being aware of the impact of, for example, the environment, it is essential that we have the ability to form and develop a relationship that can communicate interest, concern and empathy to an older person. Older people with high support needs may have a lived experience in which their concerns and difficulties are overlooked or marginalised, or they may feel afraid that if they complain, their situation will worsen and services and people in which they rely will be withdrawn. The skills in assessment and interviewing discussed in Chapter 5 are also relevant in respect to working positively with a person to enable them to tell their story in their own way or to identify issues that are a priority or of concern to them.

Research by O'Keefe and her colleagues (2007) confirmed the serious and long-term impact that the experience of abuse had on older participants. Some participants experienced permanent changes in their relationships with a family member as a result of the abuse they experienced. Others experienced emotional conse- quences, including anxiety, worry and long-term distress.

It is crucial that safeguarding plans do not fall into the same trap as traditional approaches to care planning for older people; that is, providing 'care' but failing to address issues such as emotional distress. Social workers are well placed to offer interventions to help older people move forward from the distress and disruption caused by an abusive relationship. Alternatively, if an older person is in severe emotional distress, they could be referred to a specialist counselling service or to mental health support services.

Recording and writing skills

Recording skills are critical in safeguarding and any investigation of possible abuse. Healy and Mulholland (2009: 68) have identified the purposes of record keeping as:

- Providing a vital information base for work with a service user/s.
- Clarifying the case situation for the social worker and service user/s.
- Making the social work/social element of the case visible.
- Promoting opportunities for collaboration and collaborative responses.
- Promoting the recognition of good practice.
- Providing a vital information base for the achievement of consistency in social work interventions.
- Being a basis for evaluation, monitoring and review.

As in all social work contexts, good record-keeping skills are para- mount. The inadequacy of case records has been identified as an issue in child protection inquiries and record keeping was a major area of inadequacy in 45 public inquiries into child deaths between 1993 and 1994 (Trevithick, 2005: 249). Social workers have not always received adequate and effective training in record- keeping skills (Pritchard and Leslie, 2011) and the importance of record keeping can get side-lined. It is worth noting that record keeping is *not* a matter of satisfying yet another procedure or regulation; effective records can help practitioners gain insights into the work they are doing by giving a 'sense of distance from the spoken events of the case which can enable you to recognise more easily the implications of what has occurred, to state clearly the focus of events, and to emphasize the issues, problems and needs that they contain' (Healy and Mulholland, 2009: 74). Good record keeping constitutes a key professional activity.

Point for reflection

- How would you define a good case record?

Healy and Mulholland identify a good case record as one that is focused, factual and evidence based, accessible and concise (2009: 75). What other forms of written record or document are commonly used in safeguarding practice?

In a safeguarding investigation that involves court proceedings, case records and other written materials may well be used as evidence and so they *must* be of a standard acceptable to the court in order to avoid them being discarded as irrelevant (Pritchard and Leslie, 2011) and to prevent the risk of censure as an individual practitioner as well for the social work profession. Case conferences require reports of the investigation and should be produced in line with agency requirements to promote consistency in reporting processes. Conference reports should be checked by line managers or supervisors to ensure that they are produced to a satisfactory standard and includes an appropriate level of information, evidence, analysis and discussion.

Safeguarding plans should be a multi-agency response, developed with the service user. A safeguarding plan addresses the risk of abuse or actual abuse that has occurred, giving clear and detailed information about how services, support structures and interventions will aim to minimise harm and promote recovery from abuse (ADASS, 2005). The plan should also include information about how the plan is being monitored, by whom and with what purpose, as well as a date for a formal review. Pritchard and Leslie (2011: 168) have commented that safeguarding plans are often insufficiently detailed and do not evidence what workers and organisations are doing. Similar to other plans, a safeguarding plan should identify:

- The objectives of the plan.
- Who is involved and why.
- What individuals or organisations will do, to what purpose and when.
- How the plan will be monitored.
- When the plan will be reviewed.

It is imperative both that safeguarding practice works within a values framework where the person at risk or who has experienced abuse is always kept at the centre of practitioner activity and that interventions do not do any of the following:

- Victimise a service user (for example, effectively 'removing' an older person from their home by encouraging them to go to a care home for respite care if the cause of their harm or risk of harm can be dealt with or managed in another way).
- Make a service user's situation worse than it is already (for example, heightening the person's risk of harm or actual harm by poor or unresponsive practice; encouraging interventions that inappropriately limit a service user's rights to independence or security and safety).
- Use interventions that do not fit the level of potential or actual harm (that is, the interventions are too minimal and do not offer protection or interventions that are paternalistic).
- Take into account the feelings, wishes and aspirations of the older person.

Developing skill and knowledge in safeguarding practice

Safeguarding practice is an issue for *all* practitioners, regardless of their role and experience. However, the investigation of safeguarding referrals requires the development of specific knowledge and skills, which are achieved via ongoing professional development, such as participation in action learning sets; reading relevant articles; attending 'Making Research Count' events; participating in mandatory and practice-focused training; supervision and leadership support; learning from colleagues; and the development of practice experience. Specialist knowledge will include:

- Preserving and presenting evidence.
- Court craft.

- Interviewing and evidentiary requirements.
- Specialist communication skills.
- Report writing and participation in case conferences.
- Risk assessment and risk-management skills.
- Use of the law (for example, criminal justice law).

Practice focus

What is your responsibility?

You are at a care home to undertake a planned review. You have arrived a little early and a number of people are eating lunch. You notice two people in the sitting room in armchairs, with lunch on the table in front of them. The tables are pulled up tight to the chest of each person, a man and a woman. The woman's walking stick is out of reach from where she is sitting. The man has lost his slipper and appears to have slid down in the armchair in an attempt to reach his slipper or get out of the armchair. As you start to make sense of the scene, a care worker approaches the gentleman and, shaking him roughly by the arm, says, in an apparently irritated manner, 'Oh, for goodness' sake, Mr Jones', pulls the table away from him and removes his dinner. Mr Jones, clearly startled, starts to cry.

- What would you do if you were faced with this situation?

Social workers have a responsibility under their Code of Conduct (General Social Care Council, 2010) to ensure that appropriate procedures and processes are used to 'Challenge and report dangerous, abusive, discriminatory or exploitative behaviour and practice' (para. 3.1), as well as to inform an employer or appropriate authority where the practice of a colleague or colleagues may be unsafe or adversely affect standards of care (para. 3.4). The *No Secrets* guidance also highlights the importance of staff acting on suspicion or evidence of any abuse or neglect and passing concerns on to a responsible person or agency (Department of Health, 2000: 6.2). In situations of this kind it is imperative that the registered manager is informed about the incident (or the identified person in charge), as well as the social worker informing their own manager at the earliest opportunity. The manager should record the incident and take steps to ensure that appropriate action is taken to investigate the event and take any immediate actions that might be required to protect the resident as well as other residents from harm.

Safeguarding and personalisation

The growth in personalisation in England has led to concern that people using direct payments would be at risk of abuse from personal assistants, who were not subjected to the same level of scrutiny that is commonplace in formal agencies. Moreover, there has been concern that the emphasis on individualised services, underpinned by independence, personal choice and individual outcomes, has resulted in risk being transferred from the state to the individual (e.g. Scourfield, 2007). While the available research highlights considerable benefit in employing personal support assistants via direct payments, some concern has been expressed that those assistants may work longer hours than they are paid for and that boundaries and roles may become blurred (e.g. Leece, 2010).

Supporters of personalisation argue that the use of direct payments ensures a focus on outcomes that can help to identify any potential risks involved. Thus the discussion focuses on how best to achieve the outcomes a person wants to achieve and, at the same time, to work with identified risks to ameliorate them. This, it is argued, will ensure that safeguarding becomes an integral part of personalisation rather than safeguarding and personalisation running in parallel to each other (Littlechild *et al.*, 2011: 171).

Box 4.4 Personalisation and safeguarding

Duffy and Gillespie (2009) have highlighted the ways in which traditional responses to need, via community care services, have served to exacerbate and create risk of abuse:

- *Self-determination* – I am at greater risk of abuse if I cannot direct my life, if I cannot communicate and if I am not listened to.
- *Direction* – I am at greater risk of abuse if my life does not suit my preferences or character and if I am perceived by others as lacking social value.
- *Money* – I am at greater risk of abuse if I lack money or if I cannot control my own money.
- *Home* – I am at greater risk of abuse if I cannot control who I live with and who comes into my home and if I cannot protect my privacy.
- *Support* – I am at greater risk of abuse if I have no one to help me and if I cannot control who helps me.

- *Community life* – I am at greater risk of abuse if I am not part of my community, if people do not know me and I have no chance to contribute to it.
- *Rights* – I am at greater risk of abuse if there is no publicly understood and enforced protection for me from the abuse of my rights.

Five points are identified during which risks can be specifically discussed with a service user who will use direct payments to secure their support needs:

- *First contact* with the local authority should mean that everyone involved is alert to the possibility of a person being at risk of harm and is able to respond appropriately.
- *Assessment* with support from practitioners to assess their needs and apply for a budget offers a clear opportunity to identify risks, and to act when the situation requires it.
- *Capacity* involves identifying whether a person has capacity to make critical decisions about self-directed care.
- *Support planning* is carried out by the person themselves and potential risk can be identified and responded to in the development of a support plan.
- *Plan reviewed* by the local authority, which can offer constructive suggestions and potentially reject the plans. This is a time when discussion of potential risk factors can take place as well as evaluating the effectiveness of the steps taken to address them.

It is clear that an outcome-focused approach has the potential to address a wider definition of risk: for example, the risks caused by factors such as loneliness. Clearly, there is a need to ensure that those people who need it receive support in identifying risks and working out the best way to achieve identified outcomes, as well as in acknowledging and addressing the risks. Reviewing outcomes offers a further opportunity to consider potential risk and local authorities need to develop consistent policies towards risk assessment, management and risk taking and supporting complex cases (Littlechild *et al.*, 2011). How, for example, can risk be appropriately addressed in the context of direct payments for a person with a fluctuating condition that may change rapidly and without notice? What are the potential consequences for service users and for local authorities who are accused of failing to provide adequate finance to meet identified outcomes? What are the ethical issues for a local authority providing direct payments to support a service user who chooses to remain in an abusive and dangerous situation?

There is clearly more work to do in terms of developing appropriate responses to critical questions about risk. The prevention agenda is a key element in the *No Secrets* guidance and has remained high on the government's policy agenda (e.g. Department of Health, 2010a). However, most councils continue to provide services (or finances) to those people in the highest bands of eligibility. This can create specific risks for people who are screened out of services on the grounds that they do not meet the eligibility criteria, as well as having the potential to overlook the risk of harm that is already present for those people (Brown, 2009; Tanner, 2010).

Putting it into practice

1 How is risk assessed and managed in the context of direct payments in your workplace (or practice learning agency)?
2 How might local authorities respond to the call to develop preventative services in light of the current emphasis on responding to people who have only the highest levels of need?
3 What ongoing forms of support are available to social workers in your agency to develop their professional skills and knowledge base in safeguarding practice?

Further resources

Penhale, B. and Parker, J. (2008) *Working with Vulnerable Adults*, Abingdon: Routledge.
Unpicks practice knowledge and skills in working with vulnerable adults.

Pritchard, J. and Leslie, S. (2011) *Recording Skills in Safeguarding Adults: Best Practice and Evidential Requirements*, London: Jessica Kingsley.
This book offers an important opportunity for practitioners to examine and understand the role of recording in safeguarding. Using case examples, activities and opportunities for reflection, it invites the reader to participate in developing their recording skills in this critical area of practice.

Scragg, T. and Mantell, A. (2011) (eds) *Safeguarding Adults in Social Work*, 2nd edn, Exeter: Learning Matters.
An edited collection with useful chapters on the Mental Capacity Act, serious case reviews and developing user-focused communication skills.

Action on Elder Abuse, www.elderabuse.org.uk
Awareness-raising website with a helpline service and commentary on current policy, legislative reform and information leaflets about abuse.

In Control, www.in-control.org.uk
A national charity that aims to ensure that people who need support have the right and freedom to control that support. The website has information on community networks, campaigns, reports, responses to policy and research.

PART II

Practice Issues

CHAPTER 5

Practice skills and values

CHAPTER OVERVIEW
- Social workers cannot bestow empowerment on people who use services; rather, they may help to create relationships or environments in which an older person may feel empowered.
- Social workers have a crucial role to play in advocating for a person who uses services, or in enabling a person to access independent advocacy support.
- The skills and attributes of effective communication are an essential foundation to forming and developing effective relationships between the social worker and the older person and their wider network, as well as in inter-professional working.
- Maintaining an 'open' approach when working with older people, underpinned by an understanding of the diversity of older age and experiences of ageing, is essential to good practice.

Introduction: Core skills and values

This chapter considers some of the core skills and values relevant to social work with older people. Empowerment is a much-used term in all areas of social care and there is a critical debate as to its purpose and application in social work. This chapter argues that social work skills must embrace and include a commitment to facilitating the possibility of empowerment; moreover, that it is essential to challenging oppressive practice with older people. Effective and skilled communication constitutes a fundamental attribute in forming and developing relationships, working in partnership and in multi-agency contexts. This chapter introduces key issues in communication in a social work or helping context, which are drawn on throughout the book. Linked to communication, the chapter considers the importance of skills such as advocacy in social work with older people.

Inequality, empowerment and social justice

As we saw in Part I, a historical stress on a medical model (high-lighting the biological dimensions of ageing) created the potential to emphasise dysfunction in older people (Westerhof and Tulle, 2007). The medical model reinforced a commonly held assumption or myth that all older people would inevitably decline into ill-health, disability and cognitive impairment (with the associated costs to services that such a 'burden' would impose). Second, it set in place a tendency to treat older people with disabilities and impairments as experiencing nothing more than could be expected 'at their age'. The result is that older people may be denied services or support from which they might benefit. This is one root cause of age-based discrimination in health and, indeed, similar issues can be traced in the historical development of social care.

As long ago as 1998, Means and Smith highlighted the paucity of imaginative policy and service response to older people with long-term illness and disability. The tendency to focus on institu-tional care prevailed through a considerable part of the twentieth century and community care services were consistently slow to develop. Historically, social care services for older people have been arranged on the basis that qualified staff are not involved in assessment and intervention. There has been a tendency, rather, to think about older people as an essentially homogenous group who need little more than 'care' drawn from a limited range of 'off-the-peg' services. Implicit in this response is the assumption that prac-tice with older people did not particularly require social workers to possess up-to-date theory and knowledge, and a relevant skill and value base.

Age-based discrimination

Older people who use services may be particularly susceptible to age-based discrimination. Ageism may be experienced at individ-ual, organisational/institutional and societal levels (e.g. Thompson, 2006). At an individual level, a person may use language that is derogatory about an older person; this includes professional people who may, for example, construe personality traits such as assertive behaviour as 'stubbornness' or 'fierce independence'. On an organisational level, older people may be offered services that are inferior when compared to services provided to other people who require personal social services. On a societal level, older people do not, for example, have access to a mobility component in Attendance Allowance in the same way that a younger disabled person might have via the Disability Living Allowance.

What should be an appropriate agenda for anti-oppressive social work practice with older people? Social work practice and values should, as an underpinning principle, aim to provide appropriate and sensitive services by responding to need regardless of the social status of the person (Dominelli, 2009).

Anti-oppressive practice requires practitioners to challenge traditional notions of professionalism where, for example, the 'expert' (the social worker) may exert power over the other (the older person). People in power have access to valued resources, knowledge and information and may exert power in a way that demonstrates and reinforces the power imbalance. Such a person:

- Chooses what information and knowledge to share, with whom and when.
- Has a notion of themselves as an 'expert', e.g. as knowing more about the older person than the person does.
- Makes decisions independently and without the active involvement of the person.
- Engages with procedural or administrative assessment and intervention.
- Is uncreative and will use 'off-the-peg' solutions even if there is evidence that this may be unworkable or unsuitable.
- Wants to be listened to, but neither listens nor hears.
- Is unaware of the nature of structural oppression.
- Uses the language of power, e.g. jargon, technical language, insistence on written communication.
- Takes little effort to make information accessible.
- Solely 'calls the shots' in terms of when and how the intervention and professional relationship take place, what they consist of and how long they last.
- Behaves in a manner that communicates a belief that older people are all essentially the same.

Social workers must be able to reflect on and analyse their practice in the context of the power they have and in conjunction with the older person's position and context (Ray *et al.*, 2009). This emphasises an interest in and commitment to process in the social work relationship, together with a commitment to participatory and inclusive practice and social justice. The implications of participatory and partnership practice mean going beyond a tendency to assume that the location of problems inevitably rests with the older person, characterised by simple labels ('depressed', 'demented', 'frail woman'). We should guard against analysis polarising people into particular attributes, which Laird (2008) has identified as a form of 'essentialism'. Instead, a broader approach should encompass analysis of the impacts of, for example, the environment in which an older person lives; their social and emotional relationships; their access to resources; and the potential impact of life course inequalities.

We should not assume that age or being 'old' is the defining experience for a person. Gender, race and ethnic identity, sexual identity, professional identity, the experience of living with a long-term illness, experiences of inequality or access to economic resources may be as or more relevant to a service user's identity than their chronological age. Analysis of an older person's individual context invites us to consider, for example, the possible impact of poverty over the life course and the ways in which gender and age cross-cut this experience to sharpen economic inequality.

Empowerment and older people

There is much talk of empowerment in social work; indeed, it would be almost impossible to pick up a social work textbook without finding significant reference to it (for a full discussion, see, for example, Fook, 2002; Higham, 2006). Fook (2002: 103) argues that modernist perspectives on empowerment tend to view power as 'possessed' rather than 'exercised'. Moreover, Fook goes on to argue that empowerment of one group of people (for example social workers) over another group of people (for example older people) may in itself be disempowering because it involves labelling a group 'disempowered'. To further illustrate this point, Lymbery (2005: 134) comments:

> it is by no means uncommon to read the work of students who claim to 'have empowered x by y'! In reality, empowerment is not a commodity that a social worker can transfer to a service user, but rather a condition that a service user is able to achieve.

Social workers may have a role in enhancing the potential for an older person to act with agency and assertiveness about their desired outcomes. However, in the context of organisational constraints and where practitioners are required to work within the policies and procedures of the agency, the degree to which a culture of empowerment can be promoted when service users often cannot determine what is or is not provided and have no opportunity for 'exit' from a service is questionable (e.g. Lymbery, 2005). Ultimately, the struggle for changes in power structures is affected by for example, the collective efforts of people who use services. Bartlett and O'Connor (2010), for example, highlight the collective efforts of people living with dementia to challenge discrimination and stigma and the impact that a collective voice has had in asserting human rights and a political voice.

Increasingly, critical practice in social work, among other disciplines, has recognised the importance of locating empowerment in the context of citizenship (e.g. Clark, 2009). The person as citizen is reflected as an underpinning principle in the disabled people movement (e.g. Duffy and Gillespie, 2009). Thinking about the network of people surrounding social work (older people, professionals, carers and dependants) as fellow citizens highlights that we are all protected and obligated by shared rights and duties of citizenship (Clark, 2009: 49). In their work focusing on broadening the theoretical perspectives in dementia, Bartlett and O'Connor (2010: 37) have argued the importance of social citizenship as an underpinning concept, defined as:

> a relationship, practice or status, in which a person with dementia is entitled to experience freedom from discrimination, and to have opportunities to grow and participate in life to the fullest extent possible. It involves justice, recognition of social positions and the upholding of personhood, rights and a fluid degree of responsibility for shaping events at a personal and societal level.

Practice underpinned by social citizenship as defined by Bartlett and O'Connor (2010: 70) is informed by key principles, including:

- Active participation in one's own life and wider society that is valued, supported and encouraged.
- Potential for growth and positivity.
- Connection between individual experience and circumstances and broader social and political structures and cultural contexts.

- The importance of a collective community fostering a sense of solidarity.

While these principles are identified in relation to people living with dementia, they are relevant to the experience of older people with high support needs who too often are overlooked or marginalised by professional services (e.g. Blood, 2010) and have almost no collective voice.

Point for reflection

- How do you respond to the principles identified as underpinning a social citizenship approach when thinking about an older person with high support needs?
- How do or might these principles inform your practice with older people with high support needs?

Communication skills

Effective communication is central to all social work practice. Forming, developing and maintaining relationships; working in situations of stress and uncertainty; working with people who are struggling with loss and bereavement; helping people to assess their needs; assessing decision making capacity; planning and undertaking interventions; signposting people to resources; helping people to find ways to use individual budgets to purchase support needs; negotiating with other agencies and professionals; and many other responsibilities and activities could not be undertaken without an awareness of the complex factors that influence communication and the ability to communicate effectively. Practitioners need to recognise and understand the complex and multiple individual, psychological, emotional, social, cultural, political and environmental factors that influence communication.

They must engage with the complex task of recognising the factors that might influence a person's communication when using services and adjust their own communication style and approaches accordingly.

It is impossible to be absolutely prescriptive about how to communicate effectively with individual people. Each person you meet will have their own unique life history, evidenced by different attitudes, values, coping strategies, diversity in social networks, cultural norms and family practices. Moreover, each person may have communication needs caused by factors such as sensory impairment. This highlights both the complexity of appropriate engagement and relationship building and the importance of approaching social work interviews with an open and 'not knowing' approach (Glaister, 2010). The practice role focuses on finding communication styles and approaches that feel right for the practitioner and, more importantly, meet the needs of the individual older person and the tasks at hand. As a foundation, the skills involved in counselling approaches are considered to be fundamental to relationship building, effective communication, interviewing and intervention (Trevithick, 2005).

There are a range of theoretical orientations that inform counselling approaches, but most are underpinned by the following:

- Non-judgemental attitude
- Unconditional positive regard
- Empathic understanding
- Genuineness
- Trust
- Confidentiality
- Active listening

Assessment should be concerned with working together in order to:

- Develop a shared understanding of a person's views, aspirations and hoped-for outcomes that is built on a recognition that individual people are expert about their own situation, as well as taking account of the views of other people in the person's network.
- Identify the strengths and resources that a person has or potentially has, as well as their coping strategies and emotional reactions to current difficulties.
- Examine significant changes and their bearing on current circumstances.
- Seek the professional input of others as required.
- Develop a reasoned response, with the primary aim of meeting the outcomes identified.
- Ensure that any subsequent goals of intervention are written down so that they may be evaluated after an agreed period of time.

It is perhaps easy for us to under-estimate the complexity of the messages that we have to communicate to service users. Individual budgets, eligibility criteria, the role of different professionals, charging arrangements for different types of support and the detail of support plans are aspects of work that practitioners undertake every day. But to an older person, they may all seem bewildering, frightening and offputting. We have an obligation to try to do all we can to avoid jargon and to ensure we are 'speaking clearly, at moderate volume, at moderate tempo, with little hesitancy, without undue fidgeting, nervous laughter or throat clearing' (Kadushin, 1990: 281). This is not always easy in situations of high emotion that require complex evaluations, information sharing and decision making.

Howe (2008) highlights the importance of emotional intelligence in the context of inter-personal communication. First of all, social workers must be able to cope with and manage the stresses associated with working with older people who are often in difficult, stressful and upsetting situations. Second, we must be able to reflect on our own communication and the practice that goes with it. Third, we must be able to use those reflections as a means of developing and improving practice.

Similarly, we should not under-estimate the skill involved in switching our communication styles and approaches to meet the demands of the diverse and often complex and changeful situations that are encountered in social work with older people. While there may be many situations in which we feel we can communicate with ease and confidence, there will be others where our confidence falters or we feel anxious or uncertain of the demands that will be placed on us. The situations that cause anxiety will vary from person to person. Trevithick (2005: 117), for example, highlights the communication challenges associated for many of us with talking to people in senior positions or whom we perceive and experience as more powerful:

> My guess is that most social workers feel more comfortable talking to service users than people in senior positions and our feelings can give valuable insight into how people who use services may feel about discussing their circumstances with social workers and other professionals.

Developing self-awareness through reflection, supervision and peer feedback can highlight areas of communication that might be difficult and show how we might address them.

Social workers need to approach communication with older people from a value position that each person is a unique individual.

What does this mean in practice? As a first base, thinking about social work practice with older people as working 'with the elderly' or in 'care of the elderly' can communicate a message, to oneself and to others, that older women and men are a group who are essentially all the same, rather than individual people with unique biographies, life histories and circumstances.

Initial meetings: The importance of preparation

A proactive practitioner is likely to prepare and plan for the initial meeting. Allen and Langford (2008: 79) highlight the importance of preparation as a key factor in improving the chances of an interview meeting both the service user's and the social worker's objectives. A social worker is likely to have information about the reason for referral and so may begin to ponder who else might need to be involved in the assessment process, as well as identifying who is already involved; they may consider what information they need to have to hand or whether particular requirements, such as an interpreter, are indicated. These considerations constitute appropriate planning, but it is equally important that practitioners keep an open mind about the person and their needs.

Proper preparation for a meeting is quite different from assuming that this is an assessment with a specific set of outcomes or actions that have already been 'decided'. Such an approach may serve to reinforce stereotyped assumptions and close down the possibility of creative responses to a person's circumstances or really listening to what sorts of outcomes the older person hopes to achieve. It runs the risk not only of dehumanising the older person, but of marginalising the real skill of social work. Social work should not be about bureaucratic compliance and maintaining the status quo at all costs.

Milner and O'Byrne (2009) have emphasised that basing assessment on discriminatory stereotypes, similar to the examples cited here, inevitably creates barriers and will affect the quality and outcome of the encounter and, most importantly, the experience for the older person. Assessments, interventions or, indeed, any dialogue based on this approach to practice are informed by power imbalances and are at the root of social injustice (Milner and O'Byrne, 2009: 33). An approach to practice that marginalises the voice of the older person in favour of determining eligibility for a service, for example, is likely to be evidenced by communication approaches that include maintaining control over who speaks and in what order a person's 'story' is told; controlling the topics of talk; making assumptions before all of the information is gathered; and listening that focuses on identifying factors to determine eligibility rather than the emotional response of the person to their situation.

A practitioner committed to creating environments and practices to encourage genuine participation must acknowledge the existence of a power imbalance and also how their practice approach can contribute to addressing such an imbalance. Assessments, in which the professional assumes control and expertise at the expense of the service user, also mean that there is a real danger that the practitioner will fail to understand the nature of the person's need; the older person may feel disempowered by not feeling listened to, respected or of interest to the assessor. This approach constitutes oppressive practice and will not contribute in any meaningful way to enabling an older person to engage actively in their own assessment of need or in co-producing an assessment.

Asking questions

Kadushin (1990) 'unpicks' the ways in which a social worker's approach to questioning can be experienced as helpful and purposeful to a service user by enabling him or her to explore their current situation as well as their responses, coping strategies and preferred outcomes. Unhelpful questions can include leading or suggestive forms of questioning, which may, for example, encourage a service user to agree with the social worker about the best or most appropriate route or service. Evidence tells us that older people with high support needs who live in care homes rarely felt that they were the instigators of the move to the home. Rather more often, older people identify professional workers as the instigators in their move (e.g. Bowers *et al.*, 2009).

Point for reflection

- In what ways can different types of question be unhelpful in an interview situation?

Too many yes/no questions are responses to 'closed' questions (those that require a limited and fixed answer such as 'yes' or 'no'). However, they do have an important place in communication. For example, they can be very useful to verify factual information. Sometimes, they can be helpful when working with a person in extreme emotion who finds free expression impossible (e.g. Trevithick, 2005). Closed questions can also have an important place when working with people with communication difficulties. For example, a person with dementia and associated memory difficulties may find it hard to respond to some open-ended questions, but may handle a question that requires a 'yes' or 'no' response. Nevertheless, too many closed questions may communicate the message that you are not interested in the person's story and may prevent you as an assessor from really understanding the nature of the person's situation. There is a particular danger that assessment tools based on independence in activities of daily living can be presented as a list of questions rather than a conversation.

Practice focus

Questions

Mr Samuels has support at home to help him with washing and dressing in the morning. He has some assistance from family to shop and pay bills and uses a combination of cook-chill meals and family-prepared meals that he heats in a microwave. He is managing to get to the toilet and at night time uses a commode, which is situated close to his bed. Recently, Mr Samuels has found it harder to get to the toilet in time and feels the need to pass urine many times during the day. He is worried and very embarrassed about his difficulties. A social worker has visited to review the care he is receiving.

SOCIAL WORKER: So can you get to the toilet OK?
MR SAMUELS: Yes.
SOCIAL WORKER: Good. And um, do you, um, know when you need to, um, go?
MR SAMUELS: Yes.
SOCIAL WORKER: So, um, you don't have 'accidents' then?
MR SAMUELS: No.

While the answers that Mr Samuels gave were inaccurate, the line of questioning from the social worker effectively prevented him from being able to express his concerns or worries. A more open-ended and flexible flow of conversation may have enabled Mr Samuels to talk about what was concerning him and support him by making a referral for medical advice.

Garbled or unclear questions can be difficult to overcome when, for example, emotions are running high or when difficult questions are being asked. They are unhelpful to an older person who, rather than locating the fault with the practitioner, may feel foolish for not being able to understand what is being asked. A person who is anxious to cooperate may respond to unclear questions in a way that does not accurately reflect their situation in an attempt to 'get it right'.

Double or multiple questions can cause confusion because the person may not always know which part of the question to respond to, for example:

> Where shall we meet, we can stay here, or we could go to the day room, or if you like, I could go and ask the nurse if there is a side room we could go in. What would you like?

Such questions can be particularly difficult for a person with memory difficulties or someone who is anxious, distressed, in pain or where emotions are running high. It is easy to feel overwhelmed by too much information, to forget what was asked and simply feel unable to respond. As a result, assumptions about the person can be made that are simply inaccurate. There is a danger that the social worker's problems in communicating sensitively and appropriately become the older person's problem!

Too many 'why' questions can feel accusatory. A person with dementia may be particularly susceptible to feeling overwhelmed by 'why' questions if they have an impaired working memory and are unable to recall the information required. The result may be that they feel embarrassed, upset or withdrawn and, in the worst case, are inappropriately 'labelled'. The social worker's poor communication skills can become the older person's problem:

SOCIAL WORKER: Why do you think that your daughter has asked me to come and see you, do you know?
OLDER PERSON: Um.
SOCIAL WORKER: Well, she was worried that you were trying to collect your pension when the post office was closed and everyone was in bed. Why do you think that was?
OLDER PERSON: Um.

These issues can all be exacerbated by a social worker failing to observe aspects of behaviour such as signs of social discomfort or distress, or 'outpacing' the person in communication by talking too quickly (Morris and Morris, 2010).

Listening skills

Hearing is a physiological act, while listening is a cerebral act that can only be developed through practice. In order to listen, social workers must be able to demonstrate genuine interest in their encounter with the person, actively seek to understand the world from the perspective of the older person, and be aware of the importance of non-verbal communication in communicating meaning. Communication skills, such as relevant follow-up using open questions, reflection, paraphrasing and non-verbal communication, can tell a person that their story and the information they are giving are important and are being closely attended to.

Active listening involves the practitioner paying close attention to the service user, but also communicating to them that they *are* being listened to (e.g. Trevithick, 2005). It is a demanding skill, as it requires practitioners to focus on listening rather than allowing their mind to drift off into other thoughts; this can be a tall order for a busy social worker. It is also demanding because it requires us to achieve a balance between questions that promote active, appropriate and purposeful information gathering, listening to the person and giving information – which is often complex – in an accessible and inclusive way (this is discussed in more detail in Chapter 6).

Non-verbal communication

Non-verbal communication may be regarded as the interpreter of verbal communication by telling us

> something about the validity of the message, its urgency, whether it is being sent humorously, seriously, sarcastically ... It says something about the person's attitude toward the message ... Non-verbal communication says something about the speaker's relationship with the listener ... They help us interpret the message we are hearing ... Verbal communication is concerned with 'what' we communicate; non-verbal communication is more concerned with 'how' we communicate. (Kadushin, 1990: 269)

For a fuller discussion of non-verbal communication in an interview situation, see Kadushin, 1990; Trevithick, 2005; Koprowska, 2011.

The role of non-verbal communication in interaction is fundamental to us all, but thinking about non-verbal communication in respect of older people may reveal particular considerations that with forethought, planning and observation can be addressed to avoid the person being disadvantaged. An older person may have significant sensory impairment, which can have a crucial impact on their ability to participate in verbal communication on a one-to-one basis or in collective or group settings (Evans and Whittaker, 2010). It is important for a practitioner to be aware of these issues and also of the potential solutions to them.

It might simply suffice to establish whether the person usually wears a hearing aid. If they do, then it makes sense, if they appear to have difficulty hearing, to ask them if they need any assistance with their hearing aid. It is essential to check whether the hearing aid is fitted (correctly), in the correct ear, switched on and with a functional battery. This may sound self-evident and too basic to waste words on, but it is common to find older people who have hearing aids with batteries that need replacing, who have misplaced their hearing aid or who have an unrecognised hearing impairment. Allen *et al.* (2003) demonstrated a significant reduction in disability among people with dementia living in care homes when they were screened for hearing loss, and given treatment and/or prescribed hearing aids.

Eye contact is an important non-verbal behaviour in terms of its ability to communicate interest, attention, involvement and concern. Kadushin (1990) has highlighted the fact that eye contact, along with all non-verbal behaviour, is culturally mediated and may not be desirable when a person is communicating something that they feel is embarrassing or when their composure is threatened. Eye contact may also be avoided if the person does not want to see the reaction of the recipient of communication. These issues need to be borne in mind when talking one to one, especially if the talk is on issues that the person feels uncomfortable about or sensitive issues are being discussed.

It is also important to consider that an older person may not have full access to the usual range of non-verbal behaviours as a result of physical or cognitive impairment. For example, a person who is blind will not use eye contact in the same way that a sighted person would; a person with hemiplegia resulting from a stroke will not have access to the usual range of hand and arm movements; a person with chronic pain may limit their movements to reduce pain; a person with depression may appear withdrawn and exhibit few physical movements or present as anxious, with rapid movements, gestures and pressured speech.

Social workers can communicate distance or engagement by how near the other person they sit. Like eye contact, proximity is culturally mediated and influenced by context, but physical distance between people is significant in any interview encounter. Thompson states that 'if we stand too far away, we will come across as, quite literally too distant' (2003: 126). Again, however, the individual circumstances of an older person may mean that the usual rules of proximity do not apply. A person who is in bed or who has a severe hearing impairment may require that we sit closer than might be considered usual in order to enhance their hearing and participation in the conversation. A person with complex needs in dementia may prefer us to move more closely into their personal space in order to maximise their potential to engage and respond. These strategies have to be used with sensitivity; it would be wrong to assume, for example, that a person with dementia will necessarily feel comfortable with someone sitting inside a personal space usually reserved for people with whom they have a closer or intimate relationship.

Special communication needs

Older people from minority ethnic groups may need translation and interpreting services. There are good reasons why family members may not be the appropriate people to offer this help.

Family members may feel uncomfortable communicating sensitive or personal questions and information to or about a member of their family. Cross-gender interpreting may demand discussion of topics that are embarrassing or very sensitive if raised between men and women. It may also be difficult for a family member, with their own needs and feelings, to interpret without bias. This may be particularly pertinent for a person providing care and support to someone with complex needs when they are themselves feeling exhausted and under pressure or where there may be safeguarding concerns. Under these circumstances, social workers must understand the complexities and pressures and work with professional interpreters.

At other times, an older person may have communication difficulties caused by, for example, a stroke. In this context, it may be relevant to work with family members or speech and language therapists in order to obtain advice and information about the most appropriate way to facilitate the older person's participation. What should never be acceptable is to *assume* that communication with the older person is 'impossible' and to rely on family members because it is quicker or avoids potentially complex encounters with the person. Once again, there is often a balance to be achieved between ensuring that an older person is kept at the centre of the picture, but also not overloading them if they are unwell, tired, in pain or anxious. As well as being sensitive to the ways in which a person communicates, social workers need to use their practice knowledge and wisdom together with sensitive observation skills.

Written communication

Finally, the issue of written communication is a vital component of social work practice and should not be overlooked or side-lined. Record keeping is an essential professional skill and should summarise facts, evidence, decisions, action taken, evaluation and monitoring/review information (Healy and Mulholland, 2009). Service users have the right to see their files and what is written about them and this right is laid out in the Data Protection Act, 1998. There are some exceptions as to what can be shared and social workers and students on placement should be familiar with the policy of their agency. It is now commonplace for agencies to have computer systems providing, for example, information about service users, a record of involvement with the person, the input of other agencies and current care and support going to that person. Increasingly, attention and resources are being given to computerised systems that are compatible with those of other agencies and this is clearly an important component in effective partnership and multi-agency working. Social work practitioners must be familiar with the use of these systems as well as, increasingly, competent in the use of e-mail, word-processing packages, the web and other computerised internal monitoring and accounting systems.

Plans for care should be written with clarity, stating the purpose of the intervention, what will happen, by whom and over what period. They should avoid jargon. Reports should be constructed to the standard required by the agency. It is important to consider the purpose of the report, as this may influence its content, style and structure. For example, a report for a safeguarding conference about an adult at risk is likely to require a summary of issues identified from multi-disciplinary assessment and/or investigation; evidence; risk factors; information as to the person's strengths, resources and individual context; and recommendations of appropriate courses of action or intervention to safeguard the person. It is also good practice for the older person to be aware of and as far as possible to have participated actively in the construction of the report (see Chapter 4).

Letters to service users should be written clearly and concisely. It is certainly the case that some older people have been badly frightened by the quasi-legal tenor of letters about, for example, reviews of care arrangements. Actively thinking about and planning for a service user's communication needs can prevent them feeling that their needs are unimportant or have been disregarded. A letter written in a small typeface, for example, may be of little use to an older person with macular degeneration. There is a legislative basis that requires us to ensure that agency procedures do not make it impossible or very difficult for a person with disabilities to make use of a service offered by that agency (Disability Discrimination Act, 1995, Section 21).

Negotiating skills and advocacy

A key skill in social work is negotiation. The purpose of negotiation is to reach some form of agreement, perhaps among a range of options or to resolve a disagreement, conflict or injustice (e.g. Coulshed and Orme, 2006). Thompson (2009) has highlighted negotiation skills as being essential in promoting shared decision making and partnership. Negotiation forms an important part of direct work with older people, for example in exploring and agreeing potential options for support and intervention. While it is essential that the older person is kept at the centre of the picture, it is also highly likely that negotiations will extend beyond the person to other key people in the system, such as:

- Family and friends, including carers, who may have different needs and different agendas.
- Potential providers (for example personal assistants, community groups, voluntary agencies, housing facilities).
- Other professionals and agencies involved or likely to be involved in specialist assessments, interventions and the ongoing support of the person.
- Other departments within the organisation (for example resource allocation panels, safeguarding team, duty workers, finance departments).

While this list could easily be extended, it highlights the complexity of negotiating and communicating with a number of people in the system as well as keeping the older person involved in and/or informed of progress. It is possible that different people will have different views about what is needed or required and this will often make the negotiation more complex. A social worker may be supporting an older person to access an individual budget to provide support at home; a community nurse may feel that the person should be admitted to a care home; and the person's neighbour may be anxious that they are being asked to do more than they can reasonably cope with. You may be working with a group of people to establish the best interests of a person who does not have decision making capacity about an aspect of their care and support. Negotiation brings to the foreground the importance of multi-agency working and the fact that different knowledge, skill and value bases may lead to different analyses of risk and proposals about what is required. This, of course, may be the basis for disagreement and conflict, but it can also provide opportunities for sharing expertise, learning and mutual support in complex work.

A crucial aspect of negotiation is 'transparent practice'; that is, being open and honest in one's practice. It is appropriate to make clear to an older person what the limitations might be in respect of support services. This means that the person has the opportunity to comment about what is offered and, indeed, the right to complain from a position of information rather than being disappointed when raised expectations are not met. Transparency also communicates much about a practitioner's openness to work in partnership with the person rather than as the 'professional' who exercises their power by denying important information to service users.

Trevithick (2005) highlights the importance of acknowledging and respecting other people's points of view – even if we hope to change their mind through negotiation. This is important when working with all parts of the system, but may be particularly crucial when working with family members or agencies who may have a different view of a person's situation. The aim is to achieve a shared understanding and, to achieve this, analysis of the situation needs to be explored jointly and agreed (Payne, 2002). This means being able to listen carefully and in an *open* way to the concerns of the other person. It is possible, for example, that the older person has additional information that may change the social worker's assessment or, conversely, that the social worker has information of which another worker was not aware. Sharing information along with proposals for addressing the person's needs or responding to areas of risk are all key ways to contribute to negotiating a shared understanding. If agreement cannot be reached, then it is important to record the difference so that everyone knows what steps have been taken in an attempt to reach agreement.

There may also be times when negotiating skills are required to achieve the best outcome for an older person. Trevithick reminds us that faced with organisational constraints, defensive practice and opposition, '[r]esilience, determination and the skills of persuasion are the hallmarks of a successful negotiator' (2005: 224). Social work with older people regularly requires making a case at a resource allocation meeting; supporting an intervention that may be unpopular with others; helping older people secure their rights; and creating environments to ensure positive risk taking or that service users can speak for themselves. Many of these activities contain aspects of advocacy and may bring social workers into conflict with their employing agencies. Braye and Preston-Shoot (1995: 139) suggest that advocacy 'is designed to redress power imbalances, say between purchasers and users, by facilitating discussion of options, dissent and review of the content of negotiated agreements'.

Social workers can have a critical role in advocating for older people with high support needs by, for example, challenging responses that address support needs in standard or inadequate ways. They may help a person with communication impairment to be able to express their views, or assist someone in accessing group support via the local Alzheimer's Society. Moreover, in complex situations, or in those where an independent advocate would better serve the needs and interests of the service user, social workers can help with gaining access to an independent advocate (for example an Independent Mental Capacity Advocate; see Chapter 3).

Social workers undertaking assessment should consider their own role in advocating for older people, as well as the potential need for independent advocacy and support. Older people may not have family or friends who may act as an advocate for them or relations; the needs of a carer may mean that they cannot act independently in the best interests of the older person. Phillipson has stated:

> advocacy is important because of the likelihood of older people entering situations where their frailties may be exposed or enhanced. This may happen as older people move into residential care, or are discharged from hospital, or embark on long-term domiciliary support. (2002: 62)

Advocacy may be essential in terms of ensuring that an older person is not discriminated against on the grounds of their age, gender, class, occupational status, sexual identity and ethnic membership, and that inappropriate assumptions are not made about their mental capacity (see Chapters 2 and 3).

Advocacy has the common aim to promote the views of the individual service user, either by their own participation (self-advocacy) or by being represented by an independent advocate (citizen advocacy). (For a full review, see, for example, Payne, 2005.) Citizen advocacy schemes involve an independent advocate working with a person to secure access to resources, information or services relevant to their need. There are some examples of citizen advocacy schemes developed with older people who are particularly vulnerable to being marginalised and socially excluded (Beth Johnson Foundation, 2000).

Self-advocacy or user-led advocacy highlights the importance of service users being actively involved in defining their own needs and participating in the negotiations about how those needs might be met or addressed (Coulshed and Orme, 2006). This area of advocacy work is increasingly important in the context of personalisation, where, rather than advocating for someone about decisions made by others, advocates work with a person to enable them to make decisions about their support needs and how they are met. Older people have often been without a voice in expressing choice and preference in the way their needs are met. Breaking down professional barriers and creating practice environments where advocacy can develop is crucial and should be welcomed as part of a framework of participation and involvement in service development, commissioning and shared decision making.

Sometimes people may engage with group advocacy, when they share experiences or roles in common (Coulshed and Orme, 2006). For example, a carers' forum may provide important opportunities to ensure that carers' needs and issues are included in strategic and operational planning. Social workers may be involved in group advocacy projects with older people in other settings, such as day care or residential care facilities.

Linked to advocacy is the issue of participation and consultation in the development of services for older citizens. Øvretreit (1997) has highlighted the potentially wide continuum of involvement, from giving people information about what is going to happen to them, through to service users having responsibility for deciding on and developing services.

At an individual level, user involvement and empowerment can be promoted by recognising the importance of transparent practice, negotiated solutions, providing information, and enabling older people to access relevant and good quality support. Older people have too often been excluded from participation in wider consultation that focuses on the development of services overall. Brown and Barrett (2008) make the point that developing effective models of involvement is time-consuming and that complex organisational responses may adopt procedural models of consultation such as open days, satisfaction surveys and attendance on committees. This has a questionable impact and has been described as a consumerist approach to participation, where the main aim of the involvement is to improve the product rather than to have any significant impact on existing power relationships, organisational structures and the ways in which services are commissioned and developed (see, for example, Beresford, 2007).

Box 5.1 illustrates some of the barriers that older people, especially those with high support needs, have to overcome in order to be able to participate meaningfully in shared decision making and at the level of commissioning and developing new ways to develop services.

Box 5.1 Barriers to participation (Blood, 2010)

Attitudes and culture

- Low expectations of older people.
- Ageist assumptions about what older people want to do and are able to do.
- Fixed ideas about the sorts of services older people want and need.
- Reluctance to engage with changing power relationships.
- Lack of skill in developing participatory approaches.
- Reluctance to invest time and effort in developing participatory approaches.
- Lack of vision about what participation could/should achieve.
- Over-focus on consumer satisfaction (e.g. surveys).
- Anxiety about sharing information with people who use services.
- Belief that resource constraints make it not worthwhile.
- Assumption that older people cannot cope with bad news.

Practicalities

- Lack of transport.
- Poor access.
- Timing and duration of meetings or events.
- Lack of facilities or support to meet personal requirements.
- Lack of innovation in approaches to participation (e.g. communication).
- Poor awareness of sensory impairment.
- Lack of financial investment.
- Lack of time to invest effort in involving people with high support needs.

Creating opportunities for meaningful involvement requires organisational and cultural change and a move away from traditional, bureaucratic models of service planning and delivery towards structures at all levels of the organisation that are geared to creating empowering cultures.

Support brokerage

An older person who elects to organise their support via a direct payment may need assistance from a support broker. This is someone who supports them to work out the best way to use their estimated budget to achieve their identified outcomes. A support broker may be involved in helping a person develop a support plan, which details how a direct payment would be spent to meet their eligible social care needs (Signpost, 2011), as well as helping them identify appropriate services that they could use. Once a support plan has been worked out, it must be approved by the local authority before it can start.

Support brokerage involves the kinds of skills we have discussed in this chapter: supporting an older person to make choices and decisions; advocating for them to achieve their desired outcomes; providing information and advice about possible services and resources. Support brokers *may* be social workers, but it is a developing role and there are independent agencies who provide this kind of support as well as independent support brokers.

Multi-agency work

Social workers now operate in diverse settings and with a range of practitioners from other disciplines and backgrounds, for example in primary health care, hospitals, acute health and long-term care settings as well as drug agencies. Social workers bring vital practice skills and value to a multi-agency team committed to addressing the holistic needs of older people. Clarity about the knowledge and skills that social workers bring to a multi-agency intervention is important, alongside an openness to develop understanding of and trust in the expertise and skill that other professionals bring to the care and support of older people.

Multi-agency working implies a willingness to share skill and expertise and to develop relationships of trust where it is possible to share work without being threatened and, importantly, to debate and discuss differences of opinion. This means that social work practitioners must develop skills in advocacy, negotiation and presentation of evidence in order to contribute to the resolution of dilemmas and disagreements. Confident participation in a multi-agency setting should mean that social workers' contributions to assessment and proposed interventions should be grounded in theoretical frameworks and take account of the evidence base that informs practice (see also Chapters 4 and 7).

This chapter has addressed the basic skills required when working with older people. To practise effectively, these skills have to be underpinned by a value base embodying the dignity and value of the individual. Good communication skills are needed to convey this value base appropriately, particularly during times of assessment. It is the process of assessment to which we turn in Chapter 6.

Putting it into practice

1 Using the thumbnail sketches below, identify the sorts of communication skills you would need to use, as well as any other issues you might need to consider in your preparation for an initial meeting:

- An assessment of a person whose working memory is much reduced and who finds it hard to express herself when she feels under pressure.
- Making an assessment to judge whether someone has the decision making capacity to decide where they live.

- Helping someone to access appropriate support to receive and use an individual budget.
- Presenting a report based on a risk assessment to an adult protection case conference.
- Undertaking a joint visit where a neighbour has reported a violent incident between a mother and a son who provides care and support to her.
- Discussing the reasons why a person, in your opinion, cannot go home from hospital to a consultant who argues that she must have the bed today.
- Working with a woman in hospital who is anxious to be discharged to die at home.

2 What resources are in place in your agency to ensure that older people from minority ethnic groups receive an equal and culturally appropriate service? Can you identify any gaps in current practice and provision in your own practice setting (or a practice learning environment that you have experienced)?

Further resources

Coulshed, V. and Orme, J. (2012) *Social Work Practice*, 5th edn, Basingstoke: Palgrave Macmillan.
An essential reader for social work students.

Koprowska, J. (2010) *Communication and Interpersonal Skills in Social Work*, 2nd edn, Exeter: Learning Matters.
An interactive and up-to-date introduction to communication skills in social work.

Lishman, J. (2009) *Communication in Social Work*, Basingstoke: Palgrave Macmillan.
Builds on the previous book and offers an excellent overview of communication skills in social work.

CHAPTER 6

Interviewing and assessment

CHAPTER OVERVIEW
- Assessment in social work has long been regarded as a very important part of the social work role.
- A number of principles should underpin high-quality assessment practice: supporting the full participation of an older person in their assessment; working from a strengths perspective; systematic, reliable and valid assessments, which are informed by relevant theory.
- Sound assessment practice must be underpinned by establishing an effective relationship between the older person and social worker as well as other professionals and people involved.
- Skill in supporting participation means being aware of the negative attitudes that can pervade practice with older people, especially those with high support needs.
- Self-assessment is a growing area of interest in the personalisation agenda; however, the role of professional assessment aimed at supporting and enabling an older person to explore their situation is argued to remain critical to social work practice.

Introduction

Interviewing and its relationship to assessment in social work has long been regarded as a 'pre-eminently important activity' (Kadushin, 1990: xi). Coulshed and Orme define assessment as 'an ongoing process, in which the client participates, whose purpose is to understand people in relation to their environment; it is a basis for planning what needs to be done to maintain, improve or bring about change in the person, the environment or both' (2006: 24). Developing an understanding of the needs and circumstances of an individual older person requires a practitioner to be able to gather, organise and analyse information drawn from a potentially complex range of sources. A comprehensive assessment is likely to include:

- The older person's understanding and perception of their current needs and their hoped-for outcomes; what their priorities are; the issues and areas of need that are of most importance to them.
- Input of other people in the assessment process.
- Understanding and perception of other key people in the older person's network, for example family, friends, existing formal help.
- Structural factors, for example ethnic identity and membership, gender, culture, class.
- Biographical factors, for example personal identity; approaches to problem solving, health and illness history, information about coping strategies, assessment of continuities and changes in the person's life.
- Current strengths and resources, for example individual strengths and abilities; availability of additional resources such as support networks.
- Environmental factors, for example the ways in which the built environment may have an impact on an older person's needs.
- Risk factors and safeguarding issues.

A duty to assess a person who may be in need of services is provided for by Section 47 of the NHSCCA, 1990. Community care assessment practice, despite being identified as an assessment of 'need', has been critiqued for becoming increasingly bureaucratised and designed to test eligibility for receipt of scarce and tightly rationed personal social service resources (Glendinning, 2008). This argument, along with expressed concern about the impact of managerialist practice on the ability of social workers to use their knowledge and skill base effectively, has marginalised the importance of high-quality, professional assessment undertaken by skilful social work practitioners (Lymbery and Postle, 2010).

As discussed in Chapter 3, the current policy agenda has shifted towards the 'personalisation' of support services. Policy emphasises the importance of people having choice and control over the shape of their support, by as many people as possible being helped to access personal budgets and, wherever possible, direct payments (Department of Health, 2010a). In this context, personalisation policy has highlighted a commitment to self-assessment, arguing that this will further enhance service users' rights to exercise choice and control. Self-assessment enables a person who has support needs to complete their own assessment either independently, or with assistance perhaps from a family member, supporter or voluntary agency. The link made between assessment and gatekeeping resources or as a means of establishing eligibility has been used to add weight to the argument for self-assessment as an effective development in the independence and choice agenda (see, for example, Lymbery and Postle, 2010).

However, an argument that self-assessment is inevitably desirable and will lead to better outcomes for a person who uses services is a simplistic picture in the context of a complex, uncertain situation. It may be difficult, for example, for an older person to know how best to articulate the nature of their difficulties when they are characterised by uncertainty or changeability, as is often the case for people with high support needs. An older person may be coping with memory and other cognitive impairments caused by dementia, which will affect their ability to cope with self-assessment as well as potentially their understanding of why an assessment may be needed. Other factors, such as a sudden change in the person's circumstances caused by the ill-health or death of a carer or being at the end of their own life, will influence a person's ability or motivation to self-assess. Moreover, older people may have needs and aspirations that are in conflict with those of family members who provide support, thus making self-assessment a potentially very difficult process. There may be safeguarding or issues of risk to consider that people may need professional support to talk about or unravel.

Finally, it is imperative to recognise that the complexity of the needs of some older people will mean that personalised budgets and direct payments are neither desired nor appropriate. Lloyd (2010: 197) argues that current understandings of personalisation emphasise an instrumental view of social care, portraying services as a means of restoring people to their functions as active citizens. However, we know that older people will often only turn to social services when their support needs are high or in the period before their death. In this context Lloyd argues that ensuring that a person's needs are appropriately met in a manner that ensures their dignity and wellbeing is an ethical concern rather than a matter turning solely on notions of independence and choice.

While there will be older people for whom self-assessment will be both desirable and positive, there will also be those who will benefit from professional support in assessing their needs. This means that assessment practice must be able to respond sensitively and appropriately to older people with complex needs, who are often facing upheaval, change and transition. The aim of assessment in this context is for the process to be helpful – a service in itself – where 'the professional's knowledge and expertise can be placed at the service user's disposal, reconfiguring the nature of their relationship ... whilst retaining the primacy of the service user's understanding of their life, relationships and general circumstances (Lymbery and Postle, 2010: 2513).

This chapter is written from the view that high-quality assessment will remain an essential skill in social work practice with older people. This means working sensitively and creatively to ensure that older people with complex needs are as involved as they can be in their assessment and that it is a helpful process rather than a bureaucratic procedure. We believe that social workers have a critical role to play in ensuring that older people, who have all too often been silenced or marginalised by more powerful voices, are able to express their wishes in the context of assessment.

Key principles in assessment

How we approach assessment will in part depend on the theoretical perspective we adopt in our practice. Such frameworks will be governed by our value system, perceptions and understandings of ageing and the context and situation in which assessment is carried out, but should always be person centred and needs led, the fundamental basics of social work practice. For some this will mean taking a humanistic approach and a critical gerontological perspective (as detailed in Chapter 7), and underpinned by practice theory such as loss or bereavement, psychodynamic theory if related to earlier problems in life or an ecological approach focusing on the environment, depending on circumstances and context (McDonald, 2010). It is essential for social workers actively to consider and incorporate into their practice the social location of older people, both prior to and during assessment (Thompson, 2009).

Several key principles underpin assessment, which should:

- Be led by the person and be participatory.
- Reflect individual differences such as class, race, gender.

- Be holistic and comprehensive.
- Come from a strengths perspective.
- Be interdisciplinary.
- Be systematic, reliable and valid.
- Be informed by relevant theory, which can help to make sense of a person's situation and guide subsequent support plans and interventions.

Practice skills in assessment

The practice skills required to undertake assessment create a range of opportunities as well as dilemmas and key questions. For example, how should practitioners work in partnership with service users to create responsive and flexible support services in the context of a resource-constrained environment? How should practitioners manage the dilemma of advocating an older person's rights to personal autonomy against a backdrop of deteriorating health and potentially increasing risk? How can social workers ensure that they help an older person to identify their strengths and resources in a resource-constrained environment that may turn away assessments that look too 'positive'? How can assessment practice ensure that a person who does not wish to access direct payments or personal budgets is ensured an equal outcome?

Establishing relationships

The need to establish effective working relationships is crucial to social work. In an assessment context, practitioners need to be able to form relationships with a range of people, often in difficult, uncertain or changeful circumstances (e.g. Milner and O'Byrne, 2009).

For any interview to be successful, rapport must be established and is likely to include these elements:

- Meeting each other and making proper introductions.
- Starting where the older person is in terms of their concerns and understanding of their current situation.
- Revisiting and clarifying the reason for the meeting.
- Ensuring the best possible environment for effective communication and participation.

- Using effective inter-personal skills to demonstrate empathy, warmth, genuineness (Truak and Carkhuff, 1967), active listening and a commitment to working in partnership with the person.
- Being open-minded about what the assessment will involve and what the possible outcomes of the assessment will be.

It is often the case that an older person has not referred themselves, but instead has been referred by members of their family or workers involved in the older person's care and support. While an older person may, in principle, be agreeable to a visit from a social worker, this does not mean that they would necessarily feel confident in their understanding of what they might expect from a social worker or assessment. Evidence suggests that in the midst of a crisis, older people will often be unclear about the nature, purpose and outcome of assessment, who various professionals might be, what their role is and what help might be available (e.g. Seden, 1999).

Partnership working should permeate the whole of our involvement with an older person requesting assessment or needing help and support. This means starting with some rather basic and obvious aspects of behaviour and how we present to a service user. We have to consider the importance, for example, of being punctual (Trevithick, 2005). Kadushin has commented:

> Lateness is an expression of the difference in status between the participants of the interview. More often the low status person is kept waiting by the higher status person ... Waiting suggests to the person who is kept waiting that the person for whom she is waiting has something more important to do. (Kadushin, 1990: 270)

Social work practitioners are invariably busy, but consider what it might communicate to an older person if you are perpetually late.

It is essential that the older person knows who you are and what you are there for. The first meeting is crucial in enabling an understanding of your role and for you both to make introductions (e.g. Trevithick, 2005). Using jargon, something that often defines our professional identity or work base, is an obvious obstacle to building an effective relationship. This is not only because it may make the service user feel foolish if they do not understand what you are talking about, but also serves to reinforce the distance and power differential between service user and social worker.

Point for reflection

How do you explain the following terms to an older person with whom you are working?

- Assessment
- Eligibility criteria
- Personalisation
- Direct payments
- Safeguarding

It is clearly essential to start by asking the person to talk about their concerns or challenges rather than assuming that, as an assessor in receipt of a referral, you know as much or more about what they need. Older people may have lifelong or long-standing continuities that they wish both to highlight and to preserve. A life course approach can illustrate the way in which continuities are used to construct current identities and explain how individual older people employ strategies for managing change (Ray *et al.*, 2009). Contact from a social services team might be triggered by a sudden change in circumstances. Significant and long-standing continuities in life may have been disrupted, for example an older person might have had a fall, resulting in a loss of mobility and in their ability to manage their usual day-to-day roles and activities; or the person on whom they relied may have been taken ill or died. They may feel frightened and uncertain about their future or overwhelmed by loss. On a practical level, basic needs may be unmet and urgent support may be needed to sustain the person or to ensure their safety.

Often, social workers and social care practitioners become involved in assessing an older person as a result of their health or other aspects of their life changing over time. Assessment in this context might involve examining current support arrangements and exploring ways to adapt and amend those arrangements to continue to meet their needs. The person may wish to discuss ways to maintain important continuities, or to acknowledge the losses they may have incurred as a result of illness.

It is possible that an older person may be uncertain about the reasons for contact from social services. Someone with cognitive impairment may be unable to recall a conversation with the community nurse about a visit from a social worker and may feel defensive and upset by a perceived intrusion into their lives. It is entirely possible that a referral has been made without proper consultation or discussion with the older person, who may feel resentful or worried by the contact.

It is also likely that family, friends or other supporters may be present at a visit. It is, of course, a right for an older person to be supported by whomever they choose, and this can provide a basis for sharing information and ideas about their needs or existing support system and resources. Nevertheless, the social worker needs to be aware of the potential for other people to influence the way in which the older person responds or what is discussed:

- Supporters of the older person may have their own pressing needs or agendas.
- Some topics may be confidential or sensitive to the older person or they may not wish to discuss certain issues in front of the other person.
- A concerned friend or supporter may try to 'speak for' the older person; the possibility of this may be particularly acute when the person has communication difficulties or memory impairment.
- One family member's views may not represent other family members' and certainly not the older person's.

Clearly, undertaking an assessment with other family members or friends present may be beneficial and helpful to the older person. However, it is essential that consideration is given to the management of these potential issues. This highlights the skill required in undertaking assessments in situations that can be tense or complex.

Environments

Assessments may take place in a variety of environments, which will undoubtedly influence the experience for the older person. For example, a person being assessed at home may have 'staying put' at the forefront of their mind, whereas someone being assessed in hospital may have 'getting out' as their key outcome. An older person assessed in their own home may feel more comfortable in a familiar environment. The person's home can say much about their biography and identity and this may be a basis for developing a positive and purposeful relationship. It also serves as an important and visible reminder to practitioners of the uniqueness of this individual person. On the other hand, the person's environment may mask difficulties; for example, someone with visual impairment may be able to walk around with confidence in the familiar surroundings of their own home, but be very disorientated and uncertain elsewhere.

Observation of the person's environment and their relationship to it is immediately possible when assessment is undertaken at home. However, there are also potential pitfalls to assessment at home. While observation may give important clues about the condition of a person's home, it is important that assumptions are not made too rapidly; quick assumptions can easily be nothing more than inappropriate judgements.

An unthinking and un-reflected acceptance of our own 'standards' may lead to judgemental or oppressive practice. A practitioner may, for example, consider a person's home to be 'spotless' or clean, but if the older person has always invested care and attention in their home, or if home making has constituted a significant part of their identity and role through their life, the fact that it is no longer possible to vacuum and dust every day may be a cause of considerable worry.

Another common environment for an older person to be assessed in is hospital. This presents particular issues for the older person and for the assessor. Kadushin highlights the ways in which the status of a professional person may be reinforced in a hospital setting:

> The interviewee is lying down, the interviewer sitting or standing beside her. This accentuates status difference as does the difference between the sick and the well. The interviewer is dressed in street clothes, the interviewee in night clothes ... The interviewee is immobilized while the interviewer is mobile which once again puts the interviewee at a disadvantage. (Kadushin, 1990: 113)

It is perhaps all too easy for busy practitioners to forget that older people in hospital have lives outside of being a 'patient'. There is a danger of assessing older people as if they came into existence when they entered the practitioner's personal field of vision (Ray *et al.*, 2009) This means focusing, for example, on how an older person presents in the 'here and now'. An older person with memory difficulties may be disorientated and uncertain in an unfamiliar hospital environment, which may be exacerbated by an infection. There is compelling evidence, for example, of the impact that a hospital environment often has on the wellbeing and orientation of people with dementia and this is coupled with the potential of a systemic failure to recognise and respond to the needs of a cognitively impaired person (Royal College of Psychiatry, 2010). This can result in poor and ill-informed judgements and decisions about the person. An older person may feel disempowered and vulnerable in this situation.

There are many factors that may have to be considered in the context of assessing a person in hospital, for example they may be worried or frightened about their future. This may be critical if they have high support needs and feel concerned that people suggested they move to alternative housing, such as a care home. People in hospital may also be concerned and worried about those they have left at home; this can be particularly relevant for older spouses who provide care and support to their disabled or ill partners. Of course, people in hospital may also be fearful and worried by the diagnostic procedures and treatments they are receiving. Social work practitioners can do much to reassure older people experiencing these worries by sensitively acknowledging them and by their behaviour towards the older person, communicating respect, interest and a commitment to helping them to express their own needs, concerns and worries.

In addition, wards are often busy, open-plan spaces where achieving a degree of privacy is problematic. Assessors need to consider how they can help to create some privacy by, for example, making use of visiting rooms or side offices or considering the timing of their visit the ward. As well as issues of privacy and confidentiality, considering environmental factors can also be crucial in terms of promoting the best opportunities for effective communication if the older person has a hearing impairment, memory difficulties or multiple sensory difficulties. It can be almost impossible for a person with significant hearing impairment who also has to contend with background noise and activity to participate meaningfully in their own assessment.

A further difficulty relates to the issue of assessing need when a person is removed from their own environment. It may be the opinion of the multi-disciplinary team that an older person cannot move safely in the ward or get to the toilet independently. However, it is possible that the older person is effectively disadvantaged by difficulties in coping with the hospital environment. Corridors are wide and long; toilets may not be close at hand and they may be poorly signposted; people may be moving past the older person at speed, the older person be feeling unwell. Being 'outpaced' for older people with high support needs is likely to be a consistent feature of their lived experience (see, for example, Kitwood, 1997).

Some of the issues raised in this discussion are also likely to be relevant when assessing older people in care homes. Social workers may be need to re-assess older people living in a care home if, for example, their care needs are considered to have exceeded the level of care they are presently funded to receive. Accessing personal space for a private one-to-one discussion may, in principle, be easier to achieve, as it is most likely that the person has their own room or access to a meeting room. However, in practice it might be more complex to achieve if the person needs assistance to get about and there are no staff to help. Consideration of the best time to visit is important and some preparatory work about where a meeting could take place will save time and, most importantly, reduce stress for the older person.

Professional assessment is not about exercising professional power inappropriately, characterised, for example, by:

- Focusing on procedural assessment (i.e. checking eligibility against current priorities and against Fair Access to Care criteria) and failing to 'hear' the older person's needs, issues and concerns.
- Making assumptions about what is needed before undertaking an appropriate assessment. This approach may again be driven by the needs of the organisation (for example, to achieve a certain number of people receiving direct payments).
- Practising with assumptions informed by stereotypes. Assuming that because someone is old, they will behave in a particular way or need a particular range of services is likely to create the potential to make decisions far too early in the assessment.
- Failing to consider the importance of theoretical frameworks and appropriate knowledge bases to inform assessment practice.

While assessments are increasingly formalised in the context of assessment tools, we would argue that good assessment practice is not about proceeding through the assessment framework in a step-by-step fashion. The evidence highlights that a preoccupation with procedures will have a significant impact on the quality of the relationship that is formed and, thus, the quality of the assessment (Richards, 2000). Nevertheless, assessments should neither be unsystematic nor unfocused chats (Thompson, 2009), nor should practitioners lack detailed knowledge and understanding of the possible range of an assessment, its theoretical basis and its desired outcomes. Rather, we wish to stress the skills involved in using assessment frameworks in a way that emphasises:

- The uniqueness of each individual.
- The ability to work in partnership with individuals in an anti-discriminatory way.
- The ability to make complex decisions about the depth and range of assessment *with* the older person.
- The skills involved in analysing need, risk and desired outcomes.
- The ability to pull these factors together to move towards helping older people to gain access to support services or to be appropriately signposted to other forms of support and assistance.

An over-focus on 'the forms' may locate the expertise in a questioning model of assessment or a procedural model of assessment with the practitioner. Smale *et al.* argue that while a questioning model of assessment

> may identify basic needs, it does not address the fundamental goals of increasing choice, maintaining independence and maximising people's potential. Additional skills are needed for work with people that empowers them to have as much control over their lives as possible, and specifically enables them to exercise choice in how their needs are met. (Smale *et al.*, 2000: 133–4)

In contrast, the 'exchange model' is based on a partnership approach and starts with the premise that the individual person's views about their situation and needs are paramount. The process of defining, analysing and agreeing individual priorities is a negotiated act between the older person, the person(s) undertaking the assessment and and others in the older person's system (Smale *et al.*, 1993, 2000). An exchange model carries with it the importance of encouraging service users to identify the strengths, abilities and coping strategies that they bring to a situation of change and challenge (Saleeby, 2008). Conversely, an approach to assessment that is deficit oriented is likely to reinforce stereotyping tendencies and to promote and communicate the notion that the older person is not entirely capable of making their own decisions (Ray *et al.*, 2009).

Assessment in complex situations

This chapter has highlighted the importance of keeping an open mind about all assessments. A number of fundamental practice issues are raised when assessing and/or planning and undertaking interventions with people with dementia. For example, when is it appropriate to intervene in the life of a person with dementia? How much risk is acceptable?

Consider the practice issues that are raised in this referral received into a multi-disciplinary team based in the community:

Practice focus

Complex issues

Mrs Terrell is a widow, aged 85. Although originally from the city, she now lives in a small villa in an industrial seaside village. She and her husband met during his national service. After they married, Mr and Mrs Terrell bought the house when he was working as a nurse at the local cottage hospital. When she was 45, Mrs Terrell took a job doing a night shift as an auxiliary nurse in the same hospital. She worked there until she was 60. Mr Terrell died four years ago.

Mrs Terrell has probably had dementia for many years, but it became much more of a problem when her husband died. Her coping ability varies greatly from day to day and she does not always remember that Mr Terrell has passed away. Some days she stays in bed. She struggles to manage her personal needs and appears to have continence difficulties. She leads a very quiet life and may be depressed, having been a sociable woman much involved in the local church, which has now closed and the congregation attend the church in Seaport.

Mrs Terrell has a daughter (Jane, aged 58) in Toronto who is a head teacher and is married without children. She comes over to visit every summer and is getting more and more insistent that her mother cannot remain at home any longer. She is deeply offended by her mother's personal hygiene and has lots of arguments with the local health centre and her sister about what should be done. She insists that her mother is 'at risk' and recently has argued that Mrs Terrell does not have the mental capacity to decide where she lives.

Mrs Terrell has another daughter (Heather, aged 60) who lives in the local city of Seaport. Heather has five children and eight grandchildren and manages to combine being a dinner lady, a frequent childminder of her grandchildren and twice-weekly visits to her mother, for whom she shops and cleans. She takes the view that her mother should remain at home for as long as she wants to.

Mrs Terrell is in poor health physically, since she has late onset diabetes, which was diagnosed a couple of years ago. She had never understood the implications of this for her diet. She also has a heart condition, which necessitates water tablets as well as medication for her heart. She is not good at taking her tablets consistently. Mrs Terrell has fallen over several times recently, and although she has not been hurt, concern is increasing about her safety and lack of support.

What do you consider to be the main issues to think about in preparing to meet Mrs Terrell to assess her needs?

How would you prepare for meeting Mrs Terrell?

Post (2000) comments on the impact of living with dementia in a 'hyper-cognitive' culture where intact memory and effective cognition are fundamental to our views of 'personhood'. This emphasis is reinforced by the value we attach to the importance of independence and autonomy. It is worth reflecting on your own thoughts and assumptions about this.

Point for reflection

- To what extent do you rely on the 'usual' forms of communication when undertaking assessment?
- How does it feel to be with someone who has a disrupted working memory and difficulties communicating with the spoken word?
- How easy is it for you to change your practice to adopt other strategies that rely less on the spoken word and more on emotion, observation, non-verbal cues and other means of aiding communication such as visual cues?

A person with dementia, like anyone else, is likely to need time to build a relationship with someone who is unfamiliar to them. Of course, the need for time is especially important, given the challenges to memory and other areas of cognition that the person with dementia is likely to be experiencing. Clearly, the development of a relationship is essential if people living with dementia are to have any chance of participating meaningfully in processes such as an assessment of need and planning their support needs.

At the beginning of any assessment with someone with dementia, gaining access, particularly if the person lives alone, is crucial.

As Tibbs states, 'the social worker often has to draw on all her/his interpersonal skills and ability and use lateral thinking in order to gain entry to the house and access to the situation' (2001: 70). Imagine how a person like Mrs Terrell, with memory and other cognitive difficulties, may feel about a visit from an unknown or unfamiliar person or someone who is perceived as 'being in authority'. Feelings might include fear, anxiety, suspicion and embarrassment.

Social workers need to consider how best to approach a person living with dementia. They may, for example, consider visiting with someone who is known to the person (for example a family member or another worker involved in supporting the person); however, this would mean needing to make sure that the person living with dementia was not effectively silenced by the voice and agenda of the other person. Enriching an encounter may be enhanced by the use of visual material, such as photographs or a communicate aid, such as Talking Mats (Murphy *et al.*, 2005). What is critical is to get to know the person rather than starting the interaction with a description of an 'assessment of need'. Practice should focus on using skills to build the interaction based on how things are *at the time of the meeting*, rather than relying on the prescriptive format of an assessment tool.

Developing a relationship as a basis for understanding a person's strengths, resources and needs is crucial, especially for people with serious memory difficulties who potentially also find it harder to communicate. The emphasis on relationship does not mean that understanding and analysing needs and strengths are unimportant, however. Rather, the relationship should be built *before* making judgements about needs, strengths, risks and danger.

Clearly, practitioners need considerable inter-personal skills and the ability to use language and communication skills with sensitivity (see Chapter 5). Asking questions of a person with dementia raises particular issues. A practitioner faced with undertaking an assessment is likely to be the product of a long socialisation in the 'rules' of conversation and communication. From the perspective of the person with dementia, it is easy to imagine how stressful a range of 'how', 'why' and 'when' questions might be, particularly if there is the added anxiety of being 'investigated' or fear of being 'put in a home' or 'forced' to receive unwanted services. It is not until we bring to consciousness the issue of questions that we become aware of how much our conversation can be dominated by them, particularly when meeting someone for the first time.

The following ideas provide some suggestions for engaging with a person with dementia, although there are no absolute rules, as each person's experience and journey through dementia will be unique. It is true to say that what works well for one person may be very unhelpful with another; it is also the case that someone in early dementia is likely to require a different type of communication and engagement than someone in dementia with more complex needs. Reality orientation approaches are now considered to be unhelpful for people with complex dementia. Imagine, for example, if Mrs Terrell was confronted with the news that her husband had died every time she appeared to forget this information. A person with significant memory impairment is likely to benefit from practitioners who avoid unnecessary questions that burden their memory (Killick and Allan, 2001).

How communication starts very much depends on factors such as the person's ability to cope with new situations, how they are able to concentrate on conversation, the nature of their need and how comfortable they feel with you. However, it also rests on the practitioner. Koprowska (2011) draws attention to the importance of the practitioner being *prepared* to engage in communication with a person living with dementia. This means planning, thinking about the encounter and not assuming that it is possible to rush into the house and proceed to do an assessment by talking 'at' the person.

A good starting point could be focusing on an aspect of biography. People may be very happy to talk with you about their family and photographs are often a good source of conversation. It is possible that the person will talk about their deceased partner as if they are still alive, which can be disconcerting. A 'person-centred' philosophy asks that we start where the person with dementia starts from and that we enter their reality rather than trying to make them enter ours (e.g. Kitwood, 1997; Brooker, 2007). This means that it is not appropriate, however sensitively it is approached, to remind them that their husband/wife/partner has died. Rather, it is better to listen carefully and responsively to them and perhaps reflect back some of the emotion or content of the conversation (for example, 'he sounds like a very special man'). Kitwood (1997) has highlighted the emotional pain caused by an unthinking use of 'reality orientation' for a person who may live for some of the time in another part of their biography, whereby they are told that their partner/parent is dead and they experience the news as a fresh grief. This can, of course, happen many times a day, and if someone is stuck in a perpetual state of grief, it is hard to see how they could experience wellbeing.

It is also important that this disorientation is not assumed to be a 'permanent' and 'all-encompassing' state. A person may, for example, have reflected back on the comfort that came from the lost relationship because they were disorientated or made anxious by your visit. We can doubtless all think of times when we have clung to the familiar out of anxiety or fear of the unknown. It is possible that on another occasion the person will be be able to articulate awareness that their partner/parent has died. Even if this were *not* the case, it would be wrong to assume that they would inevitably be disorientated in every aspect of their lives or unable to demonstrate capacity about specific situations and decisions.

Other ways of beginning a conversation might focus on long-standing activities and important roles that the person is or has been involved with. For example, in the case study of Mrs Terrell, knowledge of the local church and her role as a church elder are important to her identity as well as valuing and validating her unique biography.

When questions are asked, it is essential that the person is given time to answer rather than the social worker assuming that silence is a non-response. Morris and Morris (2010) highlight how easy (and oppressive) it is to 'outpace' a person by the speed of your talk, questions and responses and even how fast you walk. A practitioner's life is often hectic and so it is important to make your own professional judgement about the need to slow down with a person living with a dementia and resist pressures from other quarters to speed up. The importance of active listening is highlighted in good practice in all assessment, support planning, wider interventions and counselling. It is vital in communication with a person with dementia. It may be that the person may appear to talk in a way that does not make sense. Killick (1994) highlights that actively listening (and not interrupting) leads to clues about the meaning and relevance of the communication to the person. It is often the case that biography plays an intensely important role in a person's attempts to communicate and should not be overlooked.

Practice focus

Biography

Joe was admitted to the assessment ward following an acute deterioration in his wellbeing and cognitive abilities. He had lived happily with his daughter for the past six years. During his stay on the ward, Joe spent a great deal of his time 'miming and acting out' a range of activities. He also often became agitated with other patients and tried to encourage them to 'get going' and 'move themselves'. He responded to the senior staff with politeness and attention, but was often dismissive of support staff.

His daughter was able to explain that Joe served in the Navy during the war and was a cook on board a submarine. It was possible to see how Joe had made sense of being in hospital by returning to this time (when perhaps he often felt frightened, out of control and could not make sense of where he was). The ward became the submarine; the patients, ratings who were clearly not pulling their weight; and the staff either senior or subordinate to Joe. His daughter confirmed that she felt his miming and acting were Joe cooking in the vessel's galley.

Assessment often involves working with a much wider system than a single person. Specialist assessments are likely to be part of comprehensive assessment and families and friends may well participate in the assessment process. Carers' assessments may also be undertaken. In addition, assessments are often conducted in family systems. It is important to consider how assessment strategies should work to include the person with dementia (who may be marginalised by people talking for them) and in addition to consider the needs and circumstances of family carers and supporters. Tibbs (2001) highlights the potential dangers of overlooking family members and their role in the family system. Carers may feel stressed or anxious about their circumstances and must have time to talk about them. Carers may be facing very difficult situations and feel at the end of their tether; they may also be upset by the changes in their loved one. Practitioners often need to be clear with family members about the best way to proceed with an assessment. This does not mean railroading them into doing things 'your way', but ensuring, perhaps by clear discussion and agreement, that everyone involved can participate and contribute their views, experiences and opinions.

It is important that practitioners assessing people with dementia and their carers receive appropriate training. People with dementia have distinct needs that can easily be overlooked or completely misunderstood by an untrained practitioner. Ideally, practitioners working with people with dementia should do so regularly and work in a setting where good practice can be shared and ethical or practice dilemmas discussed.

There is a great deal of emphasis in current practice on risk assessment and risk management. Appropriate assessment and intervention to address risk are vital. However, there is a danger that the term 'at risk' can be used uncritically or on the basis of a superficial analysis of the factors that may contribute to the presence of risk. Consider, for example:

> Mr Jones is at risk in his own home.
> At risk. Needs 24-hour care.

Risk in these examples is a term that appears to require no explanation or critical analysis. Moreover, the notion of risk may be used as a shorthand note to indicate severity of need and thus secure access to finite resources. One consequence of this approach for older and vulnerable people is that being 'at risk' becomes *the* defining label and effectively outweighs other aspects that might offer a wider understanding of the person (Ray *et al.*, 2009). Kemshall comments on the impact that images of frailty and dependency have on our social construction of ageing:

> This powerful stereotype has been used to patronize and increase the dependency of older persons, and to undermine their capacity to make choices ... Choice, a central principle of community care, can be significantly undermined by professional desires to prevent risk. (Kemshall, 2002: 75)

The concept of 'risk' is far from straightforward and is, in reality, a contested and relative term. Who is at risk, and why, from what and by whose assessment? Brearley (1982) defines risk in relation to the relative variation in possible outcomes and probability, providing information about the likelihood of potential outcomes occurring. Increasingly, though, 'risk' is taken to mean danger (Kemshall and Pritchard, 1996). Titterton comments:

> in the care of vulnerable people [risk] is typically taken to mean the threat to the wellbeing or welfare of the individual, their relatives and members of the public and staff alike. The concept is often interpreted as dealing with the probability of an unfortunate event occurring. (Titterton, 2001: 219)

However, we all take risks. They are an essential part of our lives and, indeed, may be seen to contribute to our quality of life (Norman, 1985; Counsel and Care, 1993) and right to autonomy. A more balanced view of risk is called for, including potentially positive outcomes as well as potentially negative consequences.

One issue is where or how practitioners draw the line between 'acceptable' and 'unacceptable' risk. Such decisions are usually focused on an analysis of whether the person is mentally capable of making an informed choice or decision (Stevenson, 2001). The Mental Capacity Act, 2005 is intended to provide a clear statutory framework to empower and protect vulnerable people who may not be able to make their own decisions. As we saw in Chapter 3, one of the fundamental principles on which the legislation is built is a presumption of capacity. Clearly, this legislation has far-reaching consequences for assessment practice and interventions in the lives of older people for whom the ability to make decisions is identified as an issue.

The critical debate on risk highlights the potential dangers of engaging in a narrow or surface assessment of risk. For example, it is argued that the move towards managerialist practice agendas has highlighted administrative procedures and care brokerage at the expense of deeper analysis of social behaviour (Postle, 2001). Moreover, the way in which risk is constructed is likely to influence the ways in which it is engaged with, resulting in narrow assessment and intervention practice. For example, an emphasis on risk and mental health might focus on assessing the risk of danger to others and danger to self. However, people with mental health needs are likely to experience a far greater range of risks than they actually pose (Lester and Glasby, 2006).

Risk assessment in respect of older people may be influenced by the social construction of ageing, which emphasises the vulnerability of older people and potentially ageist views about the inevitable decline into dependency of very old people. Risk assessment on this basis might focus on 'paternalistic' interventions aimed at removing risk. Moreover, the location of risk with the individual may obscure structural oppressions and disadvantage that are fundamental to the experience of risk for an older person. An older person may be at risk of hypothermia because they cannot afford to pay the heating bills or at risk of loneliness and isolation because they are the last surviving member of their social and family network.

Analysis of risk also requires us to consider the fact that an older person may be at risk from the very interventions that are designed to remove risk. Pritchard (1997) highlights the real risks of living in residential care as including abuse, injury, falling, getting lost, disorientation, isolation, immobility, ill-health and death. The importance of occupational identity for people with dementia and the negative and damaging consequences of occupational poverty in care homes have also been highlighted in research (Perrin and May, 2000). This does *not* mean that interventions should never include admission to a care home or that care home environments inevitably fail to provide good-quality occupational input. Rather, the point is that assessment of risk should include a much deeper analysis, including an assessment of the potential for new risks to occur as a result of resolving the original risks.

As well as gathering information about the nature of the risk a person faces and the dangers or hazards that might promote a negative outcome, risk assessment should include consideration of the person's strengths and resources (Littlechild and Blakeney, 2001). Individual strengths and resources may provide an important basis for addressing need and risk. Risk assessment must also include evidence from other sources; family members and other professionals may have vital information to contribute to an assessment. However, it is also likely that different people will have different definitions of risk and what is acceptable; indeed, their own preferences will inevitably influence their contribution to the story. There is at least a theoretical acceptance that appropriate risk taking is desirable and that a risk-minimisation approach as a standard service response should be resisted (Davies, 1998). Interventions aimed at ameliorating the potentially negative outcomes of risk should be underpinned by evidence-based practice or by an awareness of where evidence does not exist or is of unsatisfactory quality. Moreover, practitioners should be supported by organisational frameworks that make clear the approach to risk taking and risk management. Interventions should focus on the least restrictive alternative and aim to meet the aspirations and goals of the individual service user, rather than organisational convenience or expediency. Clearly, practitioner interventions should be informed by a sound understanding of the law. Titterton comments that 'legislative provision as it exists at present tends to focus on constraint and restraint and risk is largely conceived of in a negative and constraining manner' (2001, p. 228).

Social workers are likely to encounter situations where an older person is at risk because of abuse (see Chapter 4 for further discussion on safeguarding). *No Secrets* (Department of Health, 2000) focuses on abuse as a violation of civil and/or human rights and cites categories of abuse (for example physical, emotional, sexual, financial, neglect and harassment resulting from sexist or racist abuse). Importantly, the *No Secrets* document recognises that abuse may occur in service environments such as care homes, day-care centres or other formal types of provision. The document highlights the importance of local councils, as lead agencies, developing robust multi-agency policies and practices to protect people vulnerable to abuse. Social workers should be familiar with their agency's policies on assessment and intervention in abusive situations and have received multi-agency-based training in this aspect of work. (For a full discussion of legal provisions see Brammer, 2010; for a fuller discussion of safeguarding, refer to Chapter 4.)

There are a number of further issues concerning assessments, such as who should carry out the assessment, confidentiality concerns and the content of an assessment (carers' role; breaks and social life; physical wellbeing and personal safety; relationship and mental wellbeing; care of the home; accommodation; finances; work; education and training; current practice and emotional support; wider responsibilities; future caring role; emergency/alternative arrangements; agreed outcomes and charging). Any caregiver assessment tool therefore should be designed to collect information (primarily from the carer's perspective) on different areas of the carer's situation, to analyse areas of difficulty and strength and to assess what services might best meet the needs of carers.

Conclusion: Key issues in assessment good practice

This chapter has introduced readers to a range of practice issues for consideration in assessment. Clearly, assessment is a complex activity requiring effective and skilful practice. The key issue is to produce a comprehensive understanding and analysis of the needs of a service user and their immediate support network. To achieve this, a number of skills have been highlighted, including the importance of assessment in the context of an exchange model.

Partnership work with service users requires that practitioners take seriously the importance of working with a person to understand their own perceptions and experience of their circumstances. Transparent practice means being open and honest in our dealings with service users; for example, pointing out differences of opinion in the assessment process may be difficult, but is usually preferable to trying to gloss over them. Service users require information if they are to make informed decisions about the range of choices and options open to them; social workers are well placed to provide information and also to assist older people in accessing other resources and services that may assist them. We have an ethical responsibility to ensure that the process of assessment is understood along with its range of potential outcomes for the service user and their supporters. It is these outcomes to which we turn next and discuss care and support planning, monitoring and intervention.

Putting it into practice

1 To what extent does your current assessment practice enable you to explore an older person's strengths and resources? How could you work with an older person to ensure that strengths and resources are part of your intervention/support planning?
2 What sort of preparation would you need to consider if you were planning to assess an older person who was currently staying in a care home for respite care?
3 What principles should underpin your approach to assessment of risk?

Further resources

Kemshall, H. and Wilkinson, B. (2011) (eds) *Good Practice in Assessing Risk*, London: Jessica Kingsley (Chapters 1 and 9).
This edited collection has a comprehensive range of chapters that are of interest to a wide range of social work, social care and health care practitioners.

Milner J. and O'Byrne P. (2010) *Assessment in Social Work*, 3rd edn., Basingstoke: Palgrave.
Explores in detail the theoretical approaches, principles and practice skills required in assessment.

Morris, G. and Morris J. (2010) *The Dementia Care Workbook*, Maidenhead: Open University Press/McGraw-Hill.
An interactive text for people interested in developing their knowledge and practice base with people living with dementia.

Dementia Services Development Centre, Stirling University, www.dementia.stir.ac.uk
A host of information on further training in dementia care, including publications, research reports and the Dementia Services Development Centre's newsletter.

British Society of Gerontology, www.britishgerontology.org
Information about membership, conferences and other events, including the society's annual conference.

The King's Fund, www.kingsfund.org.uk
Commentary on current national policy, including personalisation and direct payments. The website also carries comprehensive and useful reading lists on various topics of interest to social work students and practitioners.

CHAPTER 7

Planning support and care, interventions and review

CHAPTER OVERVIEW

- In identifying how a person's support needs are met, there has been a shift in emphasis from care plans to support plans.
- Support plans are outcome focused and specify how a direct payment or individual budget is being spent.
- Support plans should record any particular risks and detail the strategies in place for the person to be able to manage those risks.
- Thinking about individual needs and analysing those needs remains an important part of the process.
- Social work interventions are informed by a wide range of theoretical perspectives and practice models.
- Social work with older people should include interventions that are aimed at enhancing wellbeing or quality of life.
- It is important to recognise that older people have needs or difficulties, as with people at any other part of the life course, which may not be improved by 'practical services'.

Introduction

This chapter considers how assessments of need are translated into agreed plans that confirm how a person's identified and eligible needs will be met. Traditionally, a service user's needs, together with the services that were provided to meet those needs, were recorded on a care plan. More recently, the term 'support plan' has been used to record the changes or outcomes that a person wants to achieve with a direct payment. However, a service user may elect for services to be organised partially or completely by the local authority. In this event, it is still likely that needs and outcomes will be recorded on a support plan. Support plans should identify important information about the person, the goals and outcomes that will be addressed, and what changes will be made to achieve those outcomes. If the service user has elected to receive a direct payment, the support plan will also specify how that person will use the money to achieve the outcomes. As well as providing an explanation of what is being attempted to address an individual's identified outcomes, a support plan also forms the basis for evaluating the outcomes. It may be completed by a service user independently or with help from an independent broker, by a social worker, by another supporter or with a mix of support.

This chapter discusses the role and importance of personalised support plans. There is a need to ensure that support plans are linked to identified needs and outcomes developed from an assessment. The importance of ensuring that support plans can be reviewed or evaluated is also considered.

The chapter also looks at direct social work interventions such as crisis intervention, task-centred work, cognitive behavioural approaches, counselling, networking and working with carers. This list is not exhaustive, but aims to give the reader a flavour of the strengths and weaknesses and the contexts in which such interventions operate.

Underpinning this chapter is the conviction that interventions must respond to the diversity of older people's lives. This represents a significant challenge in practice environments, which have increasingly focused on providing care services to meet needs considered essential for basic survival. In this context, Hughes warned of the dangers of care managers becoming 'a mechanism for the exploitative rationing of insufficient resources' (1995: 102). Negotiating and implementing interventions, services and resources and helping an older person to identify how best to meet their needs are complex tasks. Planning and developing an intervention and subsequent plan, therefore, should not simply be a matter of pulling a range of goods 'off the shelf' and applying them to the life of an older person, regardless of their individual biography or needs and what their own aspirations or preferences might be for how those needs are addressed. The circumstances of Mrs Terrell, whom we met in Chapter 6, highlight a potentially complex system populated by family members, other professionals and agencies with different ideas about how her needs should be addressed.

Practice focus

Planning and preparing for discharge from hospital

Mrs Terrell has been in hospital for almost two weeks. Her health has improved as she has been receiving medication for her diabetes and regular meals. Her wellbeing has also improved and her general mood is better. She is more active and enjoys helping with the meal trolley and coffee trays each day on the ward. This work is very familiar to Mrs Terrell, given her long history of working at the hospital; this has been very helpful in enabling her to feel settled. Her cognitive state has also improved and this is thought to be directly attributable to her diabetes being under control and eating regularly.

However, there are differences of opinion about the way in which Mrs Terrell's support should be organised and the social worker has to actively consider and work with these differences. This has involved considerable negotiation and problem solving.

Mrs Terrell is clear that she wants to continue to live at home. She has the mental capacity to make this decision as well as understand some of the implications associated with it. Although her memory is impaired, her capacity to say what she wants is clear and she retains a strong connection to her home and neighbourhood. Heather, her daughter, wants 'what's best' for her mum and feels that her mother's wishes should be respected 'if at all possible'. Jane, her second daughter, is adamant that her mother should go into a care home and that to take any other course of action would leave her mother in serious risk and danger. The medical team are of the opinion that Mrs Terrell would probably be safer and better off in a care home. However, they have supported a discharge back home and have been persuaded by the improvement in her general health and wellbeing. The team now feel that medication and diet could be controlled and sustained in her home environment if the support were there to help her.

The role of support planning

Traditionally, the means of addressing eligible needs were confirmed via a care plan. More recently, research has highlighted the importance of identifying the outcomes that a person eligible for personal social services wishes to achieve and devising support plans around their identified outcomes.

Messages from research

Outcome-focused services for older people (Glendinning *et al.*, 2006)

Outcomes are the results that support or services achieve in a person's life and are therefore personal to the aspirations and goals of individual older people. This project examined the sorts of outcomes that older people valued and wanted to achieve in respect of their own care and support needs.

Work with older people identified three groups of social care service outcomes as being key to independence and wellbeing:

Outcomes involving change

- Improvements in physical symptoms and behaviour.
- Improvements in physical functioning and mobility.
- Improvements in morale.

Outcomes involving maintenance or prevention

- Meeting basic physical needs.
- Ensuring personal safety and security.
- Having a clean and tidy home environment.
- Keeping alert and active.
- Having social contact and company, including opportunities to contribute as well as receive help.
- Having control over daily routines.

Service process outcomes (the way services are access and delivered)

- Feeling valued and respected.
- Being treated as an individual.
- Having a say in and control over services.
- Value for money.
- A good 'fit' with other sources of support.
- Compatibility with, and respect for, cultural and religious preferences.

As a matter of good practice, any intervention should be underpinned by clarity about its objectives and outcomes. Social workers who are involved in developing support plans should work with the older person to establish:

- What the person wants to achieve;
- Why;
- How they want to achieve their goals;
- What outcomes they have in mind.

An understanding of outcomes and associated goals does not mean that interventions must be inflexible and unchangeable; far from it. A clear sense of purpose in an intervention provides a basis for evaluating how successful a plan has been in achieving a person's outcomes. If there is no plan at all, or the plan is vague and general, then it is very difficult to make any comment about whether a support strategy or intervention is 'working' or not and whether any alteration or change is needed.

A support plan should confirm and provide the following:

- Agreement about the outcomes that are being addressed relating to eligible needs and the way in which they will be addressed (for example via a direct payment and how the direct payment will be used; by an individual budget that can be taken as a partial direct payment; or services secured via the local authority). This is a critical time for a service user to be able to explore their preferences in terms of ways in which needs may be met or addressed.
- Identifying specific service providers or the ways in which personal assistants, for example, will provide support. Support plans should address a range of relevant areas of the person's life. An accessibly written plan written by/or from the perspective of the person is critical in ensuring that it stays focused on the individual person's outcomes. Issues such as ways in which an aspect of risk is being addressed can also be recorded.
- Information about the amount of money provided via a direct payment or a contribution from the local authority, as well as clear information about the cost or contribution to the service user.
- Important contact information, for example information about those delivering support services.
- An opportunity to identify and clarify specifics (for example information about safe practice in moving or mobilising the person; preferences about assistance in eating; preferences and likes and dislikes; information about medication support needs; transport information).

A range of factors will shape the objectives of any intervention. Service users' aspirations, access to direct payments, views of informal carers and eligibility criteria are examples of factors that will inevitably interact and have an impact on the interventions and services that are ultimately purchased or identified. The development of an agreed course of action and intervention must ensure the participation of the service user and be underpinned by practice values that are explicit in promoting self-determination and countering discrimination. The active involvement and participation of older people in planning responses to their own needs have not been a significant preoccupation in social and health care. Failure to promote the participation of older people will nevertheless result in a danger of achieving a mechanistic definition of a limited range of needs 'solved' by an equally limited range of service solutions.

The planning of interventions and care should focus on enabling older people to be as involved as they can or wish to be in identifying, agreeing and analysing their needs and outcomes. Older people should also be assisted in finding ways to meet their needs in ways that suit them. For some people, this may mean accessing a direct payment with assistance from a support agency or other people such as family members. For others, this may not be an option that the person or family members are able or wish to consider. It should not be the case that a person who does not wish to access direct payments receives an inferior range of services.

Individual outcomes are also critical. For example, Mrs Terrell may identify the disruption to her spiritual life as a more significant issue than getting her clothes washed. It is, moreover, important that social workers, if they are helping people to identify how best to meet their needs, encourage and enable discussions with older people about their preferences in the ways in which those needs might be met. People's preferences may be influenced by long-standing continuities (for example, always eating a hot meal in the middle of the day) that they feel anxious or reluctant to change. We all have ways of doing things or personal preferences that we try to ensure are met in our own lives and homes; why should older people be an exception to this? Information about people's preferred lifestyle may give us clues about ways in which needs may be more appropriately met. For example, someone who has been and continues to be very sociable may prefer their needs to be met in a way that focuses on access to social contact (for example, a drop-in lunch facility or community church meeting rather than a solitary meal at home). It is essential to hear an older person's views about the changes they have experienced and the impacts these have on their lives. This may mean that long-standing continuities or preferences have to be amended or relinquished and new ways found to adapt to or come to terms with the change (Ray *et al.*, 2009). For example, someone with severe mobility difficulties who has always gone out a great deal in the past *may* choose to reduce this activity in order to preserve energy to continue with other important aspects of their day-to-day life.

Older people should have the opportunity to discuss the potential implications of interventions and support arrangements. For example, it is important for an older person who has not received support at home to decide on the best way to achieve this. They may need to consider the implications of not always being able to have the same support worker (taking account of leave, illness, time off) and to think about what, for them, would be acceptable and unacceptable levels of change. This means that workers who are supporting an older person to put together support plans sometimes have to have to go beyond a 'surface' discussion. This is also the case when working with older people who have complex or high levels of support need. It is not acceptable, for example, not to have a clear understanding of a person's needs concerning nutrition or the best way to get around.

Older people should also know what the costs are likely to be of any support or interventions they receive. This may after all influence the sort of help of which they wish to use. A discussion about cost and what an older person can afford may also reveal that they are not claiming their full entitlement to benefits. Helping them to claim their entitlements may, in turn, comprise an important aspect of an intervention and go some way towards improving the financial disadvantage they are experiencing. Finally, participation should also involve being honest or 'transparent' about what cannot be achieved. This can be a difficult process, as it is never easy giving bad news. Nevertheless, service users do have the right to know, for example, that they are ineligible for services within national eligibility criteria, why that is and what they might be able to do as alternative means of support or assistance.

Working in partnership with service users to identify needs and potential responses to them is also overlaid by a requirement to engage with and work with other professionals and families. Interventions to plan for Mrs Terrell's discharge from hospital will inevitably be influenced by, for example, the fact that there are a number of people who did not share the same views. The following issues are likely to be relevant when considering the system that surrounds Mrs Terrell:

- Different perspectives and opinions about the 'inevitability of dependency' in dementia. How does Mrs Terrell stay at the centre of the picture when some people may view a person with dementia as, almost inevitably, unable to give an opinion about their own life or lifestyle preferences?
- Diverse definitions and opinions about risk; what constitutes risk and whether risk taking is desirable and possible; and what degree of risk should be appropriately tolerated. What resources are available to help support Mrs Terrell in taking risks?
- Different views about the rights of individual service users to make decisions and choices about their lives; this is often made more complex by issues involved in deciding whether the person can make an informed decision.
- Who might be involved in providing support for Mrs Terrell and how those roles, responsibilities and boundaries will be negotiated.
- What might be possible and achievable in terms of creating solutions to Mrs Terrell's needs and whether these can be resourced and financed appropriately.

First of all, it is essential that interventions and associated support plans relate to the needs and circumstances identified in the person's assessment. This means that, for example, an analysis of the needs that have emerged from the assessment must be undertaken. Analysing a need in order to establish why it exists may reveal an unanticipated complexity. Consider, for example, if Mrs Terrell were to go home.

Practice focus

Analysing need

One obvious 'service solution' to Mrs Terrell's weight loss and unstable diabetes would be to use cook-chill meals or frozen food. However, analysing this area of need in an assessment suggests that this may not meet her need in an acceptable way. Consider first of all the contextual factors having an impact on Mrs Terrell's wellbeing:

- She appears to be depressed and this may act as a disincentive to eating, especially when she is alone as well as having probable difficulties in heating food up.
- Her wellbeing may be adversely affected by loss and change. The death of her husband and closure of her church may contribute to a loss of identity. In addition, of course, the loss of a lifelong partner is likely to result in no longer having someone to share a meal with and, or with, someone to prepare a meal for.
- She has lost important social, spiritual and emotional contacts with people.
- She may feel anxious, as she has to live with the realities of having memory difficulties and the challenges and disruptions that accompany these.

Mrs Terrell's cognitive impairments may affect her diet in the following ways:

- Her short-term memory is not working well and she may forget to eat meals
- There is the possibility that she will not always recall that she has meals to eat.
- If she is not always able to orientate herself in time, she may be wakeful during the night and sleep during the day, therefore not certain when to eat and, as a result, avoid eating.

If we consider Mrs Terrell as a 'whole person', the issue of nutrition becomes potentially even more complex, as can be seen in Figure 7.1.

The provision of a meal, therefore, is potentially about much more than simply receiving a hot meal each day. How, based on this deeper analysis, might Mrs Terrell's needs be addressed?

Not everyone who needs to have a nutritious and varied diet will have so many factors to consider, which highlights the importance of working with people on an individual basis.

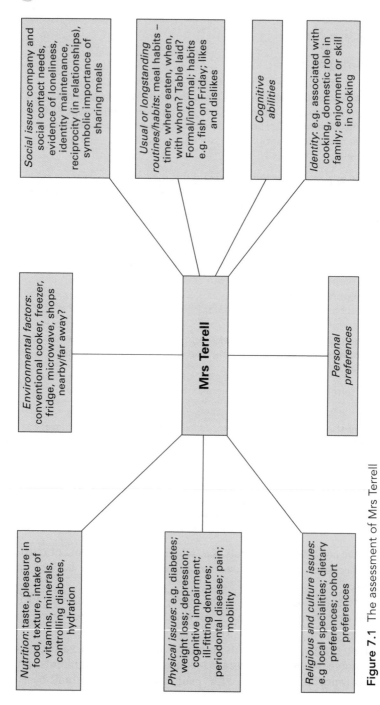

Figure 7.1 The assessment of Mrs Terrell

We should not assume that everyone's needs are due to the same issues, are of equal complexity or simplicity or may be resolved in the same way. This means coming to the analysis of need and how it may be addressed in a support plan with an open mind, rather than one that has been closed by a message that conveys to the assessor that this is a referral/assessment/care plan for a 'domiciliary care package'. Clearly, maintaining an open, critical mind is challenging when work is pressurised and creative service solutions are not easily available. Perhaps, though, in the long run, thinking carefully about the best way to respond to a person's support needs is important, if for no other reason than that it potentially saves the service user from distress, and saves the service user, social worker and others time and effort when service solutions that are clearly inappropriate go wrong or are identified as unacceptable very soon after they have been put into place.

Developing this argument further, planning interventions must also involve actively engaging with people's aspirations about their wider lifestyle. Analysis of Mrs Terrell's need for a meal might be linked to her desire to have more social contact and also to be reconnected to her religious community. Sharing food in these contexts might be of more benefit to her overall quality of life and, indeed, may resolve many of the difficulties posed by eating all of her meals at home alone. A limited analysis and an equally narrow response could fail to maximise quality of life and minimise risk; on the contrary, it may have little impact on quality of life and potentially create situations of risk – the very thing that the intervention was meant to address.

Assessments should incorporate attention to lifestyle, leisure, religious and cultural needs, as well as emotional issues. This breadth of assessment suggests, therefore, that a similar breadth must be applied when working with an older person to develop a plan of support. Moreover, Hughes argues that we should 'be open to the possibility that older people have complex emotional or relationship problems which packages of practical services alone cannot address' (1995: 112). This represents a challenge in a work environment that has increasingly tended to view older people's needs as being essentially physical and able to be adequately met by provision of services and aids. This narrow response may serve to reinforce stereotypes of older people as an inevitably dependent and homogenous group where 'one size fits all'. It is also possible that the way in which social workers do address needs will fail because other, more pressing or related needs are overlooked or ignored.

There is a legislative duty (National Assistance Act, 1948, section 29[1]) for local authorities to 'provide a social work service and such advice and support as may be needed for people in their own homes or elsewhere'. In addition, the Department of Health Guidance (DoH/Social Services Inspectorate, 1991, para. 47) states:

> the provision of advice and on-going support for clients by social workers is very important in professional terms ... the language of care management can lead to this function being under-emphasised as compared to brokering for the provision of services by third parties.

This would appear to be the case. Practitioners face the dilemma of identifying situations and circumstances in which direct work or additional one-to-one support is required, against a practice environment that does not encourage it. However, it is very difficult to work successfully or effectively with older service users where key needs are not recognised or a superficial analysis of need is utilised when a more complex approach is called for. Consider the example below.

Practice focus

Wider interventions

Mr Smith was in crisis following the death of his wife. She had been his companion for over 50 years and, more recently, had provided him with important care as his arthritis had worsened. When a social worker visited him following an urgent referral, he was unable to engage in any discussion about his own needs. He was overwhelmed with grief and also guilt as he felt he should have 'known' that his wife was going to die and done something to save her life.

The social worker, using a crisis intervention approach, identified some immediate help via a personal assistant calling each morning, but also built into the support plan up to six meetings to help Mr Smith through the early days following his wife's death. This intervention proved important in terms of helping him cope, begin to work out what he could and could not do for himself and talk about his loss and help with practical arrangements. At the end of that time, he had a support package in place and his social worker arranged to review the support after one month. Mr Smith had information about other services and resources that he might access and he knew he could contact his social worker if he needed to.

The importance of considering wider interventions beyond care brokerage is not an argument for directionless, open-ended and non-specific 'support'. Rather, it is an argument for providing individualised support that moves beyond seeing older people as being in need only of physical care. It also recognises that social workers have skills that they can put to excellent use in working with older people with complex needs, coping often with major transitions and changes and at times of considerable uncertainty.

Risk and support planning

Linked to the ability to analyse need is the importance of assessing an older person's strengths and skills, changes in their usual abilities and potential risks and dangers. Stevenson (2001) argues that risk must be analysed in conjunction with need for a number of key reasons. First, it reminds practitioners that risk may be caused or created by need and, moreover, that needs do not just happen at an individual level but also as a result of structural and institutional oppression and discrimination. For example, a person who is at risk of hypothermia in the winter may be at risk because of poor housing and poverty, which may, in turn, affect their ability to pay for heating, upgrade and refurbish their home and eat well, because local shops have closed down and transport systems have deteriorated. Linking potential risk to need should also promote active thinking about how to address risk creatively in the context of preserving a person's skill while working with the fact that their abilities may be declining. This means:

- Weighing up risk against strengths.
- Recognising that risk taking is part of life and contributes to quality of life.
- Balancing diverse opinions and perspectives.
- Negotiating possible resolutions.
- Being open in discussing observations, hypotheses, concerns and evidence.
- Having the ability to weigh up potential solutions against the potential costs to the service user and/or their informal support network.
- Being able to consider the value of potential resolutions against the resources required.
- Working within agency policy and advocating for the service user.

Table 7.1 Risks and resources

Need/Risk	Strength/Resources
Mrs Terrell is likely to be at risk from hypoglycaemic comas if she does not have access to a regular, balanced diet and medication.	Mrs Terrell has built up a relationship with home care, who have called in a couple of times a week for the past two years to help with some shopping and have often helped out by giving her some lunch. There is no reason, therefore, why this visit could not be extended to include daily visits.
Mrs Terrell has had difficulty maintaining continence during the day and also at night. This presents a significant need in terms of personal hygiene and laundry. It may present an associated risk in terms of skin care, infection and danger from slipping in urine.	Mrs Terrell has been continent during her stay in hospital. This is thought to be because she has an adequate intake of fluid each day and she is encouraged to go to the toilet for example after coffee, meal times, before bedtime. This could be included as part of a home care visit/routine. Assistance with laundry may also be built into the overall support package. Kate has hypothesised that Mrs Terrell was becoming disorientated partly because of her diabetes and also partly because she could not orientate herself in the dark to get the toilet. Kate has, therefore, investigated the possibility of fitting a 'night time guidance: finding the toilet unit', which will fade up and fade down light when pressure sensors are activated by Mrs Terrell getting out of bed. Her way will be lit to the bathroom and back to the bedroom. A regular and balanced diet may well have a positive impact on her diabetes, as will regular and appropriate dosage of medication.
Mrs Terrell does not take her diabetes medication or her water tablets.	The local chemist is happy to put the medication into a 'dosette' box and home care staff will remind Mrs Terrell to take her medication. The chemist can deliver medication to Mrs Terrell at home or, given the potential for her to decline to accept it, the medication could be collected as part of the plan. A regular visit from the specialist nurse could be arranged. This could provide important and regular monitoring of Mrs Terrell's diabetes. It is unknown how she will cope with this, as she does not know the nurse. However, she is generally well disposed to nurses given her long career as an auxiliary nurse.

Mrs Terrell misses her church and religious life and this appears to be contributing her low mood and quality of life. There is also evidence that she is most agitated during times when she would ordinarily have gone to church or been involved in church activities.	It is possible for Mrs Terrell to attend the women's group at Seatown once a week. Many of the women in this group are of Mrs Terrell's age and from a broadly similar cultural background. This is rather untried, however, as Kate cannot establish how Mrs Terrell would cope with the change or the journey (some 20 minutes away in the car). Her daughter has said that she may be able to help, but she is clearly very busy and has considerable child-care responsibilities. One possibility is to ask one of the congregation to collect Mrs Terrell in the car. Again, this is untried but may be worth attempting. Kate, as a short-term measure, has arranged home services with the vicar, who still has pastoral responsibility for the village.
Mrs Terrell has been ill at ease with her grandchildren during weekly visits to her daughter.	Kate has observed that Mrs Terrell prefers smaller groups and quieter environments. It may be possible to take one or two grandchildren to visit Mrs Terrell rather than her being faced with the whole family at one go.
Mrs Terrell has lost valued social roles as a result of the death of her husband and the closure of her church.	Kate has investigated the possibility of a volunteer visitor from the Alzheimer's Society sitting service. The idea is to work towards Mrs Terrell undertaking some sort of life story work, with a focus on village life and the history of the village.
Mrs Terrell is finding it very difficult to use the telephone.	Kate is investigating the possibility of using a picture telephone so that Mrs Terrell can call her daughter and other family simply by pressing a photograph of them. Kate has also talked about purchasing a large day and date clock.

If we consider these issues in respect of Mrs Terrell, how might a support plan be coordinated and developed to address issues of risk against her rights to autonomy and to make decisions about her own life? The social worker, in conjunction with others, had to make use of her knowledge of Mrs Terrell's wishes and aspirations, her understanding of and knowledge base for positive dementia care, her understanding of risk assessment and risk taking, and her ability to negotiate with other agencies and Mrs Terrell's family. Throughout the whole process, she would need to ensure that Mrs Terrell could say what she want to say and remained central to the process.

Table 7.1 highlights how Mrs Terrell's social worker considered needs and potential risks against strengths and potential resources.

These ideas were planned and discussed with Mrs Terrell and the team as they worked on discharge planning. Discharge arrangements were put in place with a support plan that incorporated many of these ideas.

Moving into a care home requires practitioners to record the older person's wider needs. As the home gets to know the person, they will undoubtedly develop the care plan. However, it is not acceptable to limit the initial care plan to minimal comments about physical care needs. The unsatisfactory nature of this level of care planning becomes even more pressing when the person concerned has cognitive impairment and does not, perhaps, have family members, friends or supporters who can fill in the detail. As discussed in Chapter 2, the transition to a care home can be an emotional time, involving the loss of a home, neighbours and regular routines. Social workers need to be aware of the difficulties many older people face in making this move and must not leave this emotional 'work' to relatives or care staff alone.

Reviewing support plans

The reality is that the hard work that goes into planning an intervention and developing a support plan may have to be undone or redone repeatedly and sometimes in quick succession. This may be particularly important to consider in respect of people with dementia, although is true of other people with complex, changing or uncertain situations and circumstances. It is not always possible when planning a hospital discharge, for example, to be absolutely certain how the person will cope with a particular aspect of their daily lives or, indeed, the proposed method of support or assistance. Moreover, a person's health may change and so a sudden deterioration may result in an urgent need to review, re-assess and re-define the terms of the intervention. Sometimes, situations that are uncertain, changing or have risk attached to them can be very fraught and feel difficult to manage. It is not always possible to know with certainty how to manage a situation and asking for support via supervision, opinions of other colleagues and professionals and, wherever feasible, discussing options with the older person and their family is a vital part of the decision making process.

Reviewing support plans is an essential element of evaluating the outcomes or progress made on the basis of the interventions undertaken. A review also provides the opportunity of allowing participants to stand back and reconsider whether goals should be re-adjusted in the light of experience, evaluation and reflection. On this basis, Thompson argues that reviews are critical and that we should not

> allow the pressures of work to stand in the way of reviewing and evaluating practice ... these are essential elements of good practice and so we need to use our time management and assertiveness skills to ensure that they are not 'squeezed out' by other pressures. (Thompson, 2002: 222)

Practice focus

Reviewing support plans

Mrs Terrell's care arrangements were reviewed by the community social worker. Jane had come from Canada to see her mother and was very upset that she had been discharged from hospital. She had wanted her mother to be admitted to a nursing home and felt that part of her journey to Scotland might be to make sure that her mother was moved to a care home before she returned to Canada. The review went well as it was evident that Mrs Terrell was generally doing well and that her health was consistently better. The timing of the personal assistant visiting in the morning was altered, as they were coming a little too late for Mrs Terrell.

The social worker and community nurse spent time with Mrs Terrell's daughter and they were able to explain the reasons why they were taking risks: to take some risk was beneficial to Mrs Terrell's quality of life and in achieving her desired outcome (to stay at home). Both members of staff acknowledged that they could not guarantee that Mrs Terrell's situation would not change to the point where further support or different kinds of support might be needed. Mrs Terrell's daughter was able to say something about her guilt at living in Canada and the helplessness she felt at her mother's deteriorated condition. The nurse and social worker gave her their contact details and it was agreed that she would be kept informed of any changes and that she could contact either member of staff to discuss her mother's progress.

Evaluating practice and interventions via a review process provide other important benefits. For example:

- Opportunities to learn from feedback across professional groups, thus developing practice.
- Possibilities to contribute to the evidence base by, for example, building an understanding of 'what works' in particular situations and contexts.
- Opportunities to evaluate critically whether legal powers and duties were used appropriately; organisational procedures were followed; actions were consistent with professional requirements; and the principles of good practice were pursued (Thompson, 2002).

The following key questions form a sound basis for a review:

- What were you trying to achieve?
- How were you trying to achieve it?
- How would you know when is it being achieved/was achieved?

The process of review builds on these three questions by posing further questions that can help us retain a clear focus on what we are doing and why we are doing it:

- Were the original objectives appropriate?
- Are there obstacles to achieving the outcomes?
- Were resources used to the best effect?
- Have the circumstances changed?
- Is the plan appropriate?

Addressing these questions in the context of a review should enable participants to assess the extent to which the original objectives were met or are being met, and to reach a decision about the ongoing appropriateness of the objectives and strategies used to meet them.

Older people should be helped to participate in reviewing their support needs as far as possible and based on the individual person's circumstances. Older people themselves are the experts on the degree to which their needs and outcomes are being addressed and met, how the arrangements are working, and the extent to which arrangements may need to be adjusted. Consideration needs to be given to the best ways to ensure the involvement of an older person. It might be preferential, with the permission of the service user, to gather information from other people prior to the review and then invite key people from that group to the actual review. This might prevent the pressure associated with large, formal meetings, which might provoke anxiety and, indeed, feel very intrusive. People may sometimes appreciate having an advocate with them to support them in discussing aspects of their care. This may be particularly important when local authority eligibility thresholds have changed and current care arrangements are being re-assessed (see, for example, Laird, 2011). Of course, the nature and type of a review must match the complexity of the support plan and associated arrangements.

As previously mentioned, care planning and monitoring are only one area of social work activity. Social work also has a rich repertoire of interventions aimed at helping people to change a situation that is painful or dangerous or towards improving quality of life and well-being. While there are many direct interventions that social workers will use, here we select a few for discussion that beginning social workers will experience in their practice.

Direct social work interventions

In Chapter 2 we outlined the importance of using theory as a framework for understanding and helping. In this chapter we expand on this in relation to interventions with older people, drawing on the case study material in previous chapters. We also outlined in Chapter 2 various situations and transitions that people will go through where a social worker may become involved if coping with the problem or transition becomes difficult. Inherent in the idea of transition is change; any social work intervention that accompanies transition needs to focus on enhancing the competencies a person brings to this change.

Crisis intervention

When people are unable to draw on their coping skills during times of psychological distress, crisis intervention may be appropriate. Studies have shown that such intervention has been successful in times of short-term crisis such as bereavement and loss (Rapoport, 1970) and traumatic events such as rape and domestic violence (Edlis, 1993). There are a number of ingredients in the experience of crisis, such as a precipitating event, a sense of loss, danger or humiliation, feelings of being out of control, events that may be unexpected, disruption to usual patterns and routines, and uncertainty (Parry, 1990). One of the first studies to develop the theory behind this was Lindemann, in his 1944 study of survivors of the Coconut Grove night-club fire in Boston. Reactions of sleep disorder, preoccupation with the image of the deceased, guilt, hostile reactions and a loss of patterns of conduct followed as reactions for many of the individuals who experienced grief. Those who sought help in their grief work found that they recovered in a shorter period than those who did not experience such help. Crisis intervention should therefore be time limited to the short term and should build on the coping capacities of individuals; it can draw on social work skills such as 'advocacy, bargaining, negotiation, use of empathy and appropriate challenging to achieve a constructive resolution of the crisis' (Parker and Bradley, 2010: 109).

Task-centred work

Often crisis intervention is accompanied by task-centred work. A task-centred approach, which focuses on the achievement of goals, is a practical model for social workers. It is a useful tool as small, achievable goals can be negotiated and the approach can be applied to individuals, groups and communities. Reid and Shyne (1969) and Reid and Epstein (1972) were the first to propose this method. The key ingredients of the approach are the following:

- It is time limited: it has a beginning (setting the focus and goal) and ending (reviewing).
- It is task orientated.

- It is structured.
- It has clear aims and is specific.
- It concentrates on achievable goals.
- It is systematic and appropriately flexible.
- It is measurable.
- It focuses on removing blocks to achieving change rather than searching for the 'root cause' of the difficulties being experienced.

Accompanying a task-centred approach is often a contract or written agreement between the service user and the social worker, which identifies, specifies and prioritises the task in hand, together with the time period within which it is to be accomplished, and defines who takes action and how the review of the task will be achieved.

Practice focus

Mr Smith is seriously physically impaired by Rheumatoid Arthritis and has recently moved to a flat in an Extra Care Sheltered Housing Scheme. He has found it difficult to stay in touch with his usually busy social life as the flat is located some way from his long-standing neighbourhood. Mr Smith feels frustrated and isolated and has lost confidence after coping with a difficult move and adjusting to a new environment.

Mr Smith is spending more time in his flat and appears low and unhappy. The manager of the scheme spent time with Mr Smith and realised that he needed to reconnect with old friends and perhaps try some new opportunities locally. Using a task-focused approach they identified the sorts of things that Mr Smith would like to achieve in order to feel more settled in his new home Mr Smith prioritised areas to work on and what was needed to achieve those goals. The manager helped Mr Smith to locate transport services local to the flat and some new social activities too. Over time, Mr Smith built up his network and social engagements and began to feel more settled in the flat.

Mr Smith clearly benefited from the manager's recognition that he was struggling to manage the transition as well as providing him with some support to enable him to independently achieve goals that were important to him.

Task-centred work is often part of a larger form of intervention and can complement approaches such as cognitive behavioural therapy, described in the next section.

Cognitive behavioural therapy

Different situations and events trigger different emotional responses or feelings and consequently cause different behaviour. Cognitive behavioural therapy (CBT) explores the relationship between these elements. The basic premise is that both cognitive and behavioural responses to events are based on our past experiences and what we think we ought to do in such situations, so is learned and can be changed. Change can come about by re-learning, adapting and substituting more effective responses. In older people it has been effective for treating depression and anxiety (Yost *et al.*, 1987).

CBT works best when older people actively agree to the intervention, engage in goal planning and evaluate changes (McInnes-Dittrich, 2002).

CBT involves four main stages (see for example Laidlaw, 2003; Simmons *et al.*, 2010):

1. *Preparation:*
   - Developing a relationship.
   - Focusing on what needs to be changed.
   - Discussing symptoms, causes and functioning.
   - Explaining what CBT is and assessing whether the person is suitable for this approach.
2. *Collaboration–identification.* In this phase the worker helps the person to understand the connections between situations, events and feelings. For example, Mick was very anxious about having any help to resolve some of the difficulties with his housing. He was scared, following a failed 'clean-up' in which personal possessions were lost, that any more help would only make matters worse. As a result, the situation in the house was deteriorating rapidly.
3. *Change.* In this phase the worker will work with the person to recognise any cognitive disorder in their thinking. For example, Mick was convinced that everything had to stay the same in order to keep control of the situation, even though he appreciated that things had to change as his situation was deteriorating rapidly. The worker used a number of techniques in the intervention, including written agreements, positive reinforcement strategies, rehearsal and challenging Mick's thinking.
4. *Consolidation and termination.* In this final phase changes are consolidated by a review of the older person's strengths and

new skills they may have learned as a result. Their self-awareness should then help them gain control in the future when other anxiety-provoking events arise (for a full discussion of cognitive-behavioural approaches, see, for example, Sheldon, 1995).

Counselling

The quality of the relationship between the social worker and the service user is fundamental to practice, as we have argued throughout this book, particularly where counselling is concerned. Underpinning the relationship should be familiar principles of:

- Genuineness
- Warmth
- Unconditional positive regard
- Empathy
- Trust
- Non-judgemental attitude
- Non-directive approach

Counselling can be applied in a number of settings with reference to bereavement loss and grief, traumatic past experiences, difficulties in relationships and painful transitions. Counselling skills, discussed in Chapter 3, may also be applied with a number of other approaches. Several research studies have highlighted problems between generations of older parents and their children, many of which may have been left unresolved for many years (Phillips *et al.*, 2003; Pillemar and Luscher, 2004). Role reversal may have taken place, with the carer previously the cared-for child. Caring can be a difficult task and can lead to resentment, ambivalence and abuse within relationships if stress becomes paramount.

Different members of the family will have different viewpoints on the situation under review and what the stresses are, as well as different expectations and different ways of resolving the issues. The main focus of counselling in this respect will be to encourage and support the family to 'negotiate new, mutually acceptable and agreed expectations, with each party being aware of what is expected of them and how much they can reasonably expect of others' (Scrutton, 1989: 92). This will involve encouraging family discussion, listening, identifying the tensions and interpreting them with the family in an impartial way.

Networking

One of the key skills social workers need is networking with groups and communities on behalf of service users and social services organisations. Assessing networks both in relation to informal support systems and formal support systems from the user's perspective can be a useful tool (Phillips *et al.*, 2002).

Networking draws on the theoretical underpinning of community social work and radical social work, as advocated in the 1980s in the UK. McDonald (1999) argues that networking and radical social work drew on collective action and the links between the personal and the political. Advocacy and empowerment are also part of the links between political and personal levels:

> Advocacy generally involves people making a case for themselves and advancing their own interests, or representing others and supporting them to secure and exercise their rights on an individual or collective basis. (Dunning, 2005)

Whether social workers can act as advocates is a moot point, as the prescribed roles that social workers hold through legislation and as agency gatekeepers can conflict with some definitions of advocacy, which stress the preferred wishes of the service user over the agency. However, social workers can and do use advocacy skills in their work, particularly where they are linked to focusing on achieving the outcomes defined by the older person. Until recently the focus was on the user as 'consumer' in the notion of health and social care, rather than the current shift to the focus on advocacy as citizenship. Advocacy stressing the citizenship rights of users can be empowering for older people in helping them to realise their full potential as well as rights to receive fair and equal treatment in a way which does not compromise their dignity and opportunities to preserve strengths, lifestyle and valued outcomes.

Life history work

Life history or biographical work has been used in various ways with older people. It has become an important ingredient in person-centred care for people living with a dementia.

Work with people with dementia has moved from a position of 'therapeutic nihilism' (Kitwood, 1997) to an area of practice that has undergone considerable development and change. Many of these interventions focus on maintaining and reinforcing the rights of a person with dementia to be included and feel positively engaged; to sustain emotional relationships and attachments; to feel secure; and to be communicated with in a positive and appropriate manner and most importantly, to preserve identity.

Life history work has been important in highlighting some key principles of person-centred care. Using a life history can help with developing individualised support, interventions and care planning. Knowing about a person's biography or life history can also greatly assist in making sense of aspects of their behaviour that might not be easily understandable. It is clear that workers who are aware of the life history of a person with dementia can provide positive opportunities to validate and value that person as a unique individual. Developing a life history can provide a vital tool for good-quality care. Life history work should go beyond facts about the person to include their attitudes, beliefs, values and traditions (for a full discussion, see Gibson, 2011).

Interventions with carers

In the past three decades, services and support have been developed that can enable carers to continue in their caring roles. These include the following:

- Information (about local services, financial support, nature of the illness or condition).
- Skills training.
- Emotional support (confidence building; expectations of role and valuing; someone to talk to; recognition of their own needs as individuals in their own right).
- Regular respite and domiciliary support (home adaptations, continence service, help with transport).
- Services that reflect differing racial, cultural and religious backgrounds.

However, the support for carers is not consistent. The reality is that if a service user is ineligible for support until they reach 'critical' or 'substantial' bands, carers are much more likely to experience significant physical, emotional, practical and financial consequences of their caring role. This highlights the challenge of responding in any meaningful way to the prevention agenda.

What lessons are there for social workers in this area? The National Carers' Strategy (Department of Health, 2008b) is underpinned by a number of outcomes for carers:

• Having access to individually tailored services to support their caring role.
• Having a life outside of their caring role.
• Being supported to avoid financial hardship caused by caring.
• Being supported to stay mentally, emotionally and physically healthy.
• Protecting children and young people from inappropriate caring.

The outcomes were based on direct work with informal carers, who highlighted a number of problems in their encounters with formal services. For example, they identified that assessments of need were often slow to be completed and resulted in sparse or inadequate services; financial allowances for caring were insufficient and limited; carers' own health and wellbeing is neglected in favour of their caring roles; and carers' right to a life outside of their role is neglected.

One of the priorities of the strategy is to recognise carers at an earlier stage; social work will potentially continue to have a significant role in this area of practice. What this also means for social work agencies is listening to carers; acknowledging their expertise in relationship working in partnership; looking at 'what works'; and having a supportive attitude towards carers within the organisation.

The relationship between social care organisations and carers, however, has not always been one based on a concept of citizenship. Twigg and Atkin (1994) describe models of carers based on the relationship between carers and service providers, with carers being seen by service providers as 'co-workers', 'resources', 'co-clients' or 'superseded carers'. The NHSCCA, 1990 envisaged carers as 'resources' where they provided 'free' care to support the social care system, but with subsequent Acts stressing the citizenship principle, in theory carers should be seen as co-workers. However, there is evidence (Twigg and Atkin, 1994) that such a partnership is difficult to achieve in reality and often the notion of 'co-client' is stressed, together with the needs of the carer. The 'superseded carer' is where the relationship is encouraged to become one of independence and the carer gives up the caring role.

The relationship with carers highlights the differential power relationship between social workers and informal carers, which has hampered any realistic advancement of a partnership between different agencies and carers in supporting them. Chambers and Phillips (2004) argue that this is due to several causes: the stereotyping of carers as a unified group; paternalism by health and social care workers; resource constraints; the emphasis being on the burden of care; and the multiplicity of potential partners. Nolan advocates the 'Carer as Expert' model, which should be used for the basis of assessment and intervention (Nolan *et al.*, 1998). This model takes a life course approach, focusing on the carer's experiences, and is carer centred, emphasising their strengths and coping skills.

Social workers will come across this issue in terms of working with carers not only as service users but also as employees of local councils. In a study of one local council social service, at least 10 per cent of the workforce was caring for older adults (Phillips *et al.*, 2002). Despite the agency providing social care, human resource staff had little knowledge of the numbers and profiles of their staff in relation to their caring responsibilities; staff did not know of the council's policy to support them; and much depended on individual line managers' discretion. Child care was much more acknowledged than caring for an older or disabled adult. Many staff were also reluctant to share their situation with their line manager for fear of discrimination. It is important therefore to engage in greater sensitivity to carers' needs within organisations where social workers operate as managers and as workers. Being a professional in such situations can, however, be an advantage because of the greater access to knowledge.

While the focus of this section is on carers, it must be acknowledged that for carers to be empowered, older people receiving care also need to be treated as full citizens. One of the ways in which this can be realised is by giving older people the right to choose their carer through direct payments.

Conclusion

Support planning is becoming the primary means by which a person's desired outcomes, based on eligible need, will be addressed. It provides a guide for those people involved in the care and support of a service user and, importantly, a source of reference for the service user and their family and social network. Plans should not merely focus on the physical aspects of care but also address wider outcomes, if appropriate to the person. Plans provide an important source of evaluation: have the outcomes of the plan been achieved? Identifying clearly what the goals are and how they will be worked on provides the basis for analysing why plans may be failing an older person.

This chapter has highlighted that support plans are not fixed in stone but are living and dynamic documents. Support plans will often change rapidly, especially, for example, when working with a service user who has complex and changing needs or who experiences significant risk. They also provide a vital source of reference and the potential for saying something about a service user's identity.

Putting it into practice

1 What are the goals of a support plan? How can you make sure that older people are able to determine how their support needs are met?
2 How would you address the risks that Mrs Terrell faced in developing a support plan? A care plan?

Further resources

Blood, I. (2010) *Older People with High Support Needs: How Can We Empower Them to Enjoy a Better Life?* York: Joseph Rowntree Foundation.
This research round-up provides a comprehensive review of the current state of knowledge, policy and practice with older people with high support needs. As well as highlighting the marginalisation and 'silence' of older people with high support needs, the review identifies priority areas for action and change.

Mauger, S. and Deuchars, G. (2010) *Involving Users in Commissioning Local Services*, York: Joseph Rowntree Foundation.
Highlights the importance of participation by older people at all levels of service and policy development. Examines good practice in involving people in commissioning.

May, H., Edwards, P., and Brooker, D. (2009) *Enriched Care Planning for People with Dementia*, London: Jessica Kingsley.
This provides an excellent and accessible overview to person-centred, individualised planning and support with people living with dementia.

Conclusion

In this book we have tried to demonstrate that social work with older people is an important and valuable professional role. Chapters 1 and 2 highlighted the great diversity of contexts in which people age. Social work with older people should therefore be characterised by diversity and by the unexpected, calling on well-developed social work practice skills and a knowledge base that includes a gerontological perspective and underpinned by a value base that has at its heart a commitment to challenge age-based oppression and the marginalisation of older people. The book has illustrated the reality that for many older people with high support needs, their voices are seldom heard above the more powerful voice of professional workers and others. The essence of social work is located in commitments to create conditions whereby older people can articulate their aspirations and wishes, alongside addressing factors that may have a negative impact on their lives. Older people are often faced with the need to make decisions at times of upheaval and uncertainty, along with coping with perhaps feeling unwell, being in an unfamiliar environment and with people who have assumptions or beliefs about what is 'best' for that older person. With their commitment to human rights and social justice, social workers are, at least potentially, well placed to promote the citizenship rights and human rights of older people who use services, regardless of the complexity of their needs. Nevertheless, there are considerable challenges facing the social work role with older people and it is to these that we now turn.

There has never been a 'golden age' in social work with older people and its nature and purpose have at least to some extent always been contested. There is compelling evidence that social work with adults, and older people in particular, is under-valued when compared to social work with children (e.g. Richards, 2000). Over the past two decades, the growth of care management as a means of meeting the social care needs of older people has had a major impact on the role and tasks of social workers. A managerialist approach to welfare services, characterised by increased throughput, the growth of procedural practice and the need to evidence eligibility in an environment of sparse resources, has resulted in a more administrative approach to practice (Chapter 3). There is evidence of social workers struggling to articulate the theoretical frameworks and knowledge bases on which social work practice is built, relying instead on bureaucratic systems and procedures in response to the increased demand for output and the growth of administrative imperatives (McDonald *et al.*, 2008). Similar findings were echoed in the review of the role and tasks of social work (Department of Health, 2009c), which commented that a range of factors were holding back the profession, including organisational culture and expectations of social work. Although the findings of Professor Munro relate to social work with children (she chaired the review of child protection and social work with children and families commissioned by the Secretary of State for Education in 2010), they resonate with the research relating to social work with adults, in which practice had

> evolved too far into a top-down, compliance-driven organisation. This stifled creativity and distorted priorities, with more attention given to the completion of bureaucratic tasks to specified timescales as the measure of success, than the appraisal of the quality of help received by children and their families. (Munro, 2011: 17)

With its emphasis on self-determination, human rights and working in partnership to create positive change, social work in England appears to lend itself to the growth of the personalisation agenda. However, early research suggested that social workers were not always supportive of its implementation and engaged in unilateral decision making about who might be 'suitable' for direct payments (Clark *et al.*, 2004; Ellis, 2007). A number of reasons may account for this finding, including the lack of access to effective training, especially when compared to the pace of reform (Manthorpe *et al.*, 2009: 9), and the realities of trying to navigate complex and ill-developed systems in the absence of appropriate support and organisational frameworks in the early days of reform.

These findings present a gloomy picture for the future of social work with older people in England. It seems clear that there is an urgent need to articulate the value that social work can bring to improving the quality of life for older people who use services if we are to avoid the risk of social workers being seen as irrelevant or expendable (e.g. Lymbery, 2005). Certainly, there has been a demise of social work posts in local authority teams in favour of other posts such as 'care navigator' or 'support broker', which are more likely to be occupied by unqualified staff who, presumably, cost less than a qualified practitioner. Glasby *et al.* (2011) have commented that social workers fear that the 'language' of person-alisation is being used to justify cuts to social work posts.

Nevertheless, there has been national affirmation of the impor-tance of social work with adults. The Department of Health/ADASS (2010), for example, in partnership with other agencies, indicated the potential to strengthen existing social work roles (for example assessment, support planning and review) as well as develop other roles that have not been able to flourish (for example direct social work interventions). Similarly, the Social Care Institute for Excellence (SCIE, 2010) has highlighted the simi-larities between the value base of personalisation and the value base of social work:

• Respect for the individual and self-determination, which have long been at the heart of social work and reflect the dominant value base for personalisation.
• The central role of social workers in developing and delivering personalised services to achieve better outcomes.
• The distinct contribution of social work to personalisation, with the social work emphasis on developing relationships and understanding people in their context.

We know that service users often value the skills and value base that inform effective social work practice. The National User Network (Beresford, 2007: 5) identified key skills that were valued in social workers, including advice and advocacy; negotiating with other agencies; counseling and psychotherapeutic support; sign-posting; and practical guidance and help. Research with older people to explore their perceptions and experiences of social work confirmed the value that participants placed on

> the skills and qualities of social workers whom they considered were knowledgeable about specialist services, persistent, committed, reliable and accessible, supportive, sympathetic and prepared to listen. (Manthorpe *et al.*, 2008a: 1142)

And, of course, there are the unsung heroines and heroes who, despite the many challenges, continue to find ways to deliver high-quality, effective social work services that make a difference to the lives of older people.

Putting the role of social work with older people more clearly onto the map is going to require a multi-faceted approach, but at the outset, thinking about what social work with older people is and can yet be is a vital starting point. We would argue that social work with older people should focus on the following:

- Supporting people in exploring their situations and desired outcomes through the process of co-produced assessment (Chapter 6).
- Supporting people with high support needs whose situations are likely to be complex (Chapters 2 and 6).
- Helping people to work out the best way to achieve identified outcomes (Chapters 6 and 7).
- Undertaking therapeutic interventions and wider forms of support to help older people manage complex and difficult transitions (e.g. bereavement) (Chapters 4 and 7).
- Working with older people who are at risk of, or are experiencing, harm through a range of factors, including abuse (Chapter 4).
- Challenging structural oppression, discrimination and especially age-based discrimination (Chapters 2 and 5).
- Working with other professionals and agencies to ensure that social contexts of ageing and individual older people are included as well as their voices and aspirations (Chapters 2, 4, 5 and 6).

Part of the story in raising the profile of social work with older people rests with social workers themselves. Collectively, through for example professional organisations and in their own work places, social workers may publicise the work they do and demonstrate how they have made a difference to the experience of an older person. Individually, social workers have a responsibility to embrace the importance of life-long learning and engage with post-qualification opportunities for developing their practice. New opportunities for support for newly qualified social workers as well as for a career structure in social work and post-qualification framework are emerging from the Task Force (Task Force: One year on, 2010), but social workers will also have to take responsibility for their own learning and professional development. More informally, they might be able to develop an action learning set to explore practice with older people, or have a special interest group or journal club that looks at relevant research into ageing. Social workers should consider ways to use their 'voice' and to engage in discussion and debate about developments in social work and social care policy and practice.

There is a need to develop capacity and appetite for as well as interest in social work with older people among social work students. Social work education often does not adequately address the issue of social work with older people or, indeed, age-based discrimination and ways to counter experiences of such discrimination (e.g. Manthorpe, 2010). The development of a new post-qualification framework together with higher education institutes offering programmes such as professional doctorates may, in time, contribute to the currently inadequate capacity in social work of researchers and gerontological social workers as future members of the academy.

Key social work bodies have pledged their commitment to promoting social work with adults and its distinct contribution. The Task Force implementation of recommendations, together with the development of a College of Social Work in England, may have an impact on raising the profile of social work in general and in specific areas of practice, such as work with older people.

Recently, I (Mo Ray) was talking to a team manager who was supervising work with an older person that was extremely complex. The practice involved the Mental Capacity Act, including deprivation of liberty safeguards and the use of Independent Mental Capacity Advocates and best interest decision making. Safeguarding procedures had been initiated. The work involved the older person and a large extended family who were at odds and in direct conflict about what should happen in the best interests of the older person. The team manager reflected on the difficulties he had in supervising the work, as his team was depleted of social workers. The loss of capacity in social work, in his view, had a direct impact on their ability to work positively with the situation. Local authorities must take their part in recognising the role of social work with older people in their workforce development. In the long term, a loss of capacity in social work may well have a negative impact on the lives of older people. Directors of social work have a role to play in ensuring that social work with older people remains visible and that its contribution is clear (Glasby, 2011).

This is an exciting and challenging field. It is also a field that is changing rapidly. Since the first edition of this book we have achieved a better understanding of the varied needs and situations in which older people find themselves. We can no longer view 'older people' as a homogenous group with simple needs; their lives and experiences add a complex and diverse dimension to the life course. We are also able to respond to the needs of the minority of older people who have to draw on social work services, through legislative, policy and practice developments. As professionals we need to recognise our own ageing within this and reflect on our own experiences. In this way, we hope that this book makes a solid contribution to better-informed and more confident social work.

References

Action on Hearing Loss (formerly RNID) (2009) *About Deafness and Hearing Loss*, available at http://www.actiononhearingloss.org.uk/your-hearing/about-deafness-and-hearing-loss.aspx (accessed 16 September 2011).

Adams, S. (2010) *An Ageing Population, Low Income, Home Ownership and Decay of Older Housing*, Nottingham: Care and Repair.

Age Concern (2004) *Grandparents*, London: Age Concern.

Age Concern (2007) *My Home Life: Quality of Life in Care Homes; A Review of the Literature*, London: Age Concern.

Age Concern (2008) *Information and Advice Needs of Black and Minority Ethnic Older People in England*, London: Age Concern, available at http://www.ageuk.org.uk/documents/en-gb/for-professionals/research/information%20and%20advice%20needs%20of%20bme%20older%20people%20(2008)_pro.pdf?dtrk=true (accessed 16 September 2011).

Allen, G. and Langford, D. (2008) *Effective Interviewing in Social Work and Social Care: A Practical Guide*. Basingstoke: Palgrave Macmillan.

Allen, N., Burns, A., Newton, V., Hickson, F., Ramsden, R., Rogers, J., Butler, S., Thislewaite, F. and Morris, J., (2003) The effects of improving hearing in dementia, *Age and Ageing* 32(2): 189–93.

Appleton, N. (2002) *Planning for the Majority: The Needs and Aspirations of Older People in General Housing*, York: Joseph Rowntree Trust.

Arber, S. and Ginn, J. (1991) *Gender and Later Life: A Sociological Analysis of Resources and Constraints*, Sage: London.

Arthritis Care (2007) *About Arthritis*, available at http://www.arthritis-care.org.uk/AboutArthritis (accessed 16 September 2011).

Association of Directors of Adult Social Services (2005) *Safeguarding Adults: A National Framework of Standards for Good Practice and Outcomes in Adult Protection Work*, available at http://www.adass.org.uk/images/stories/Safeguarding%20Adults/SAFEGUARDING%20ADULTS%20pdf.pdf (accessed 16 September 2011).

Asthana, S. and Halliday, J. (2006) *What Works in Tackling Health Inequalities? Pathways, Policies and Practice through the Life-Course*, Bristol: Policy Press.

Audit Commission (2000) *Forget Me Not: Developing Mental Health Services for Older People in England*, London: Audit Commission.

Banerjee, S. (2009) *The Use of Anti-psychotic Medication for People with Dementia: Time for Action*. London: Department of Health.

Bartlett, R. and O'Connor, D. (2010) *Broadening the Dementia Debate: Towards Social Citizenship*, Bristol: Policy Press.

Beeston, D. (2006) *Older People and Suicide,* West Midlands: Care Services Improvement Partnership.

Beresford, P. (2007) *The Changing Role and Tasks of Social Work from Service Users' Perspectives: A Literature Informed Discussion Paper,* London: Shaping our Lives, National User Network.

Beth Johnson Foundation (2000) *Advocacy for People with a Progressed Dementia: A Case Study in a Hospital Closure Programme,* Staffordshire: Beth Johnson Foundation.

Blood, I. (2010) *Older People with High Support Needs: A Round Up of the Evidence,* York: Joseph Rowntree Foundation, available at http://www.jrf.org.uk/publications/better-life-high-support-needs (accessed 16 September 2011).

Bowers, H., Clark, A., Crosby, G. *et al.* (2009) *Older People's Vision for Long Term Care,* York, Joseph Rowntree Foundation. Available at http://www.jrf.org.uk/sites/files/jrf/older-people-vision-for-care-full.pdf (accessed 16 September 2011).

Brammer, A. (2010) *Social Work Law* (3rd edn), Harlow: Pearson Education.

Braye, S. and Preston-Shoot, M. (1995) *Empowering Practice in Social Care,* Buckingham: Open University Press.

Brearley, C. P. (1982) *Risk and Social Work,* London: Routledge and Kegan Paul.

Brooker, D. (2007) *Person-Centred Dementia Care: Making Services Better,* London: Jessica Kingsley.

Brown, H. (2009) Safeguarding adults, in R. Adams, L. Dominelli and M. Payne (eds) *Critical Practice in Social Work* (2nd edn), Basingstoke: Palgrave Macmillan, pp. 303–11.

Brown, H. and Barrett, S. (2008) Practice with service-users, carers and their communities, in S. Fraser and S. Matthews (eds) *The Critical Practitioner in Social Work and Health Care* (2nd edn), London: Sage/Open University, pp. 43–59.

Burholt, V. and Windle, G. (2006) *The Material Resources and Well-being of Older People,* York: Joseph Rowntree Foundation.

Calasanti, T. and King, N. (2007a) Taking women's work 'like a man': Experiences of care work, *The Gerontologist* 47(4): 516–27.

Calasanti, T. and King, N. (2007b) Beware of the estrogen assault: Ideals of old manhood in anti-ageing advertisements, *Journal of Aging Studies* 21(4): 357–68.

Cameron, C. and Phillips, J. (2003) *Carework in Europe: UK Report,* London: Thomas Coram Research Institute.

Carers UK (2008) *Carers' Policy Briefing: The National Strategy for Carers,* London: Carers UK.

Carers UK (2010) *Carers UK Calls for New Social Contract*, London: Carers UK, available at http://www.carersuk.org/newsroom/item/108-carers-uk-calls-for-new-social-contract (accessed 16 September 2011).

Challis, D. J. and Hughes, J. (2002) Frail older people at the margins of care: Some recent research findings, *British Journal of Psychiatry* 180: 126–30.

Chambers, P. (2005) *Older Widows and the Life Course: Multiple Narratives of Hidden Lives*, Aldershot, Ashgate.

Chambers, P. and Phillips, J. (2004) Working across the interface of formal and informal care of older people: Partnerships between carers and service providers, in R. Carnwell and J. Buchanan (eds) *Effective Practice in Health and Social Care: Working Together*, Buckingham: Open University Press, pp. 96–110.

Clark, C. (2009) Identity, individual rights and social justice, in R. Adams, L. Dominelli and M. Payne (eds) *Critical Practice in Social Work* (2nd edn), Basingstoke: Palgrave Macmillan, pp. 43–50.

Clark, H., Gough, H. and MacFarlane, A. (2004) *'It Pays Dividends': Direct Paymnents and Older People*, Bristol: Policy Press.

Coalition on Older Homelessness (2004) *Coming of Age,* London: Coalition on Older Homelessness, available at http://www.olderhomelessness.org.uk/?pid=133 (accessed 16 September 2011).

Commision for Social Care Inspection (2007) *The State of Social Care in England 2005–6*, London: CSCI.

Commission on Funding of Care and Support (2011) *The Report of the Commission on Funding of Care and Support*, London: Commission on Funding of Care and Support.

Cooper, B. (2008) Continuing professional development: A critical approach, in S. Fraser and S. Matthews (eds) *The Critical Practitioner in Social Work and Health Care* (2nd edn), London: Open University/Sage, pp. 222–37.

Coulshed, V. and Orme, J. (2006) *Social Work Practice: An Introduction* (2nd edn), Basingstoke: Macmillan/BASW.

Counsel and Care (1993) *The Right to Take Risks*, London: Counsel and Care.

Croucher, K., Hicks, L. and Jackson, K. (2006) *Housing with Care for Later Life: A Literature Review,* York: Joseph Rowntree Foundation, available at: http://www.jrf.org.uk/publications/housing-with-care-later-life-literature-review (accessed 16 September 2011).

Davidson, K., Daly, T. and Arber, S., (2003) Exploring the social worlds of older men, in S. Arber, K. Davidson and J. Ginn (eds) *Gender and Ageing: Changing Roles and Relations,* Maidenhead: Open University Press, pp. 168–86.

Davies, C. (1998) Caregiving, carework and professional care, in A. Brechin, J. Walmsley, J. Katz and S. Peace (eds) *Care Matters: Concepts,*

Practice and Research in Health and Social Care, London: Sage, pp. 126–38.

Department for Communities and Local Government (2009) *English Housing Conditions Survey: Decent Homes and Decent Places*, London: Department for Communities and Local Government, available at: http://www.communities.gov.uk/documents/statistics/pdf/1133548.pdf (accessed 16 September 2011).

Department for Education (2010) *Building a Safe and Confident Future One Year On*, London: Department for Education.

Department of Health (1990) *National Health Service and Community Care Act*, London: HMSO.

Department of Health (2000) *No Secrets: Guidance on Developing and Implementing Multi-Agency Policies and Procedures to Protect Vulnerable Adults from Abuse*. London: HMSO.

Department of Health (2003) *Fair Access to Care Services: Guidance on Eligibility for Adult Social Care*, London: Department of Health.

Department of Health (2008a) *Transforming Social Care*, LAC Circular, LAC(DH)2008 1, London: Department of Health.

Department of Health (2008b) *Carers at the Heart of 21st Century Families and Communities: A Caring System on Your Side, a Life of Your Own*, London: Department of Health.

Department of Health (2009a) *Safeguarding Adults: Report on the Consultation of the Review of 'No Secrets'*, London: Department of Health, available at http://webarchive.nationalarchives.gov.uk/+/www.dh.gov.uk/en/Consultations/Responsestoconsultations/DH_102764 (accessed 16 September 2011).

Department of Health (2009b) *Living Well with Dementia: A National Dementia Strategy*, London: Department of Health, available at http://www.dh.gov.uk/en/Publicationsandstatistics/Publications/PublicationsPolicyAndGuidance/DH_094058 (accessed 16 September 2011).

Department of Health (2009c) *Building a Safe and Confident Future: The Final Report of the Social Work Task Force*, London: Department of Health.

Department of Health (2010a) *A Vision for Social Care: Capable Communities and Active Citizens*, London: Department of Health.

Department of Health (2010b) *Quality Outcomes for People with Dementia: Building on the Work of the National Dementia Strategy*, London: Department of Health.

Department of Health (2010c) *Prioritising Need in the Context of Putting People First: A Whole System Approach to Eligibility for Social Care – Guidance on Eligibility Criteria for Adult Social Care, England 2010*, London: Department of Health, available at http://www.dh.gov.uk/en/Publicationsandstatistics/Publications/PublicationsPolicyAndGuidance/DH_113154 (accessed 16 September 2011).

Department of Health/ADASS (2010) *The Future of Social Work in England and Wales*, London: DoH/ADASS.

Dominelli, L. (2009) Values in critical practice: Contested entities with enduring qualities, in R. Adams, L. Dominelli and M. Payne, *Critical Practice in Social Work*, Basingstoke: Palgrave Macmillan, pp. 19–32.

Duffy, S. and Gillespie, J. (2009) *Personalisation and Safeguarding*, Version 1.1, discussion paper, available at http://www.in-control.org.uk/media/52833/personalisation%20safeguarding%20discussion%20paper%20version%201.0.pdf (accessed 16 September 2011).

Dunning, A. (2005) *Information, Advice and Advocacy for Older People: Defining and Developing Services*, York: Joseph Rowntree Foundation.

Edlis, N. (1993) Rape crisis: Development of a centre in an Israeli hospital, *Social Work in Health Care* 18(3–4): 169–78.

Eisses, A. M., Kluiter, H., Jongenelis, K., Pot, A. M., Beekman, A. T. F. and Ormel, J. (2005) Care staff training in detection of depression in residential homes for the elderly, *British Journal of Psychiatry* 186: 404–9.

Ellis, K. (2007) Direct payments and social work practice: The significance of 'street level bureaucracy' in determining eligibility, *British Journal of Social Work*, 37: 405–22.

Estes, C. L., Biggs, S. and Phillipson, C. (2003) *Social Theory, Social Policy and Ageing*, Maidenhead: Open University Press.

Eurostat (2002) European Health Statistics 2002, Luxembourg: Eurostat, available at http://ec.europa.eu.

Evandrou, M. and Glaser, K. (2003) Combining work and family life: The pension penalty of caring, *Ageing and Society*, 23(5): 583–603.

Evans, M. and Whittaker, A. (2010) *Sensory Awareness and Social Work*, Exeter: Learning Matters.

Farmer, E. and Meyers, C. (2005) *Children Placed with Family and Friends: Placement Patterns and Outcomes, Executive Summary*, Bristol: DFES/University of Bristol.

Fook, J. (2002) *Social Work: Critical Theory and Practice*, London: Sage.

Foundation66 (2009) *Press Release: Epidemic of Late-Onset Drinking*, London: Foundation66, available at http://www.foundation66.org.uk/news.php/5/press-release-foundation66-highlights-epidemic-of-late-onset-drinking (accessed 16 September 2011).

Froggatt, K. (2004) *Palliative Care in Care Homes for Older People*, London: National Council for Palliative Care.

General Social Care Council (2010) *Code of Conduct for Social Care Workers* (updated), Rugby: GSCC, available at http://www.gscc.org.uk/codes/ (accessed 16 September 2011).

Gibson, F. (2011) *Reminiscence and Life Story Work: A Practice Guide*, London: Jessica Kingsley.

Glaister, A. (2010) Introducing critical practice, in S. Fraser and S. Matthews (eds) *The Critical Practitioner in Social Work and Health Care*, London: Sage/Open University Press, pp. 8–26.

Glasby, J., Dickinson, H. and Miller, R. (2011) *All in This Together? Making Best Use of Health and Social Care Resources in an Era of Austerity*, Policy paper no. 9, Birmingham: HSMC.

Glendinning, C. (2007) *Outcome-Focused Services for Older People*, Knowledge Review 13, London, Social Care Institute for Excellence.

Glendinning, C. (2008) Increasing choice and control for older and disabled people: A critical review of new developments in England, *Social Policy and Administration*, 42: 451–69.

Glendinning, C., Clarke, S. and Hare, P. (2006) *Outcomes-Focused Services for Older People*, Knowledge Review 13, Bristol: University of York/SCIE and Policy Press.

Griffiths, R. (1988) *Community Care: Agenda for Action,* London: HMSO.

Healy, K. and Mulholland, J. (2009) *Writing Skills for Social Workers,* London: Sage.

Help the Aged (2007) *What Makes a City Age Friendly?* London: Help the Aged.

Heywood, F., Oldman, C. and Means, R. (2002) *Housing and Home in Later Life*, Buckingham: Open University Press.

Higham, P. (2006) *Social Work: Introducing Professional Practice,* London: Sage.

Hirst, M. (2001) Trends in informal care in Great Britain during the 1990s, *Health and Social Care in the Community*, 9: 348–57.

Hough, M. (1995) *Anxiety about Crime Survey: First Report.* Research Study No. 147. London: Home Office.

Howe, D. (2008) *The Emotionally Intelligent Social Worker,* Basingstoke: Palgrave Macmillan.

Howse, K. (2003) *Growing Old in Prison: A Scoping Study on Older Prisoners*, London: Centre for Policy on Ageing/Prison Reform Trust.

Hughes, B. (1995) *Older People and Community Care: Critical Theory and Practice*, Buckingham: Open University Press.

Hughes, M., and Wearing, M. (2007) *Organisations and Management in Social Work,* London: Sage.

Iliffe, S. (2009) Approaches to late-life depression, *Quality in Ageing* 10(1): 9–15.

Improvement and Development Agency (2010) *Adult Safeguarding Scrutiny Guide*, London: IDeA, available at http://www.idea.gov.uk/idk/aio/19170842 (accessed 16 September 2011).

Janick, M. P., Zendell, A. and DeHaven, K. (2010) Coping with dementia and older families of adults with Down syndrome, *Dementia*, 9(3): 391–407.

Kadushin, A. (1990) *The Social Work Interview* (3rd edn), New York: Columbia University Press.

Kelly, M. (2001) Lifetime homes, in S. Peace and C. Holland (eds) *Inclusive Housing in an Ageing Society*, Bristol: Policy Press, pp. 55–76.

Kemshall, H. (2002) *Risk, Social Policy and Welfare*, Buckingham: Open University Press.

Kemshall, H. and Pritchard, J. (1996) *Good Practice in Risk Assessment and Risk Management*, London: Jessica Kingsley.

Killick, J. (1994) 'here's so much more to hear when you stop to listen to individual voices, *Journal of Dementia Care* 2(5): 16–17.

Killick, J. and Allan, K. (2001) *Communication and the Care of People with Dementia*, Buckingham: Open University Press.

King's Fund (2005) *Briefing Note: Age Discrimination in Health and Social Care*, London: King's Fund.

Kitwood, T. (1997) *Dementia Reconsidered: The Person Comes First*, Buckingham: Open University Press.

Knapp, M. and Prince, M. (2007) *Dementia UK*, London: Alzheimer's Society.

Koprowska, J. (2011) *Communication and Interpersonal Skills in Social Work*, Exeter: Learning Matters.

Laidlaw, K. (2003) *Cognitive Behaviour Therapy with Older People*, Chichester: Wiley.

Laird, S. (2008) *Anti-Oppressive Social Work: A Guide for Developing Cultural Competence*, London: Sage.

Law Commission (2010) *Adult Social Care: Summary of Consultation*, Paper 192, London: Law Commission.

Law Commission (2011) *Adult Social Care: Summary of Final Report*, London: Law Commission.

Leece, J. (2010) Paying the piper and calling the tune: Power and the direct payment relationship, *British Journal of Social Work* 40: 188–206.

Lester, H. and Glasby, J. (2006) *Mental Health Policy and Practice*, Basingstoke: Palgrave Macmillan.

Lindemann, E. (1944) Symptomatology and management of acute grief, *American Journal of Psychiatry* 101: 141–8.

Littlechild, R. and Blakeney, J. (2001) Risk and older people, in *Good Practice in Risk Assessment and Risk Management*, London: Jessica Kingsley, pp. 68–79.

Littlechild, R. and Glasby, J., with Niblett, L. and Cooper, T. (2011) Risk and personalisation, in H. Kemshall and B. Wilkinson (eds) *Good Practice in Assessing Risk: Current Knowledge, Issues and Approaches*, London: Jessica Kingsley, pp. 155–73.

Lloyd, L. (2004) Mortality and morality: Ageing and the ethic of care, *Ageing and Society* 24: 235–56.

Lloyd, L. (2010) The individual in social care: The ethics of care and the 'personalisation agenda' in service for older people in England, *Ethics and Social Welfare* 4(2): 188–200.

Lymbery, M. (2005) *Social Work with Older People*, London: Sage.

Lymbery, M. and Postle, K. (2010) Social work in the context of adult social care in England and the resultant implications for social work education, *British Journal of Social Work* 40: 2502–22.

Manthorpe, J., Moriarty, J., Rapaport, J. *et al.* (2008a) 'There are wonderful social workers but it's a lottery': Older people's views about social workers, *British Journal of Social Work* 38: 1132–50.

Manthorpe, J., Stevens, M., Rapaport, J. *et al.* (2008b) Safeguarding and system change: Early perceptions of the implications for adult protection services of the English individual budgets pilots – a qualitative study, *British Journal of Social Work* 39(8): 1465–80.

Manthorpe, J. Jacobs, S. Rapaport, J. *et al.* (2009) Training for change: Early days of individual budgets and the implications for social work and care management practice: A qualitative study of the views of trainers, *British Journal of Social Work* 39(7): 1291–305.

Martin-Matthews, A. and Keefe, J. (1995) Work and care of elderly people: Canadian perspectives, in J. Phillips (ed.) *Working Carers: International Perspectives on Working and Caring for Older People*, Aldershot: Avebury, pp. 116–39.

McDonald, A. (1999) *Understanding Community Care: A Guide for Social Workers*, Basingstoke: Macmillan.

McDonald, A. (2010) *Social Work with Older People,* Cambridge: Polity Press.

McDonald, A., Postle, K. and Dawson, C. (2008) Barriers to retaining and using professional knowledge in local authority social work practice with adults in the UK, *British Journal of Social Work* 38: 1370–87.

McInnis-Dittrich, K. (2002) *Social Work with Elders: A Biopsychosocial Approach to Assessment and Intervention*, Boston: Allen and Bacon.

Means, R., Richards, S. and Smith, R. (2003) *Community Care Policy and Practice* (3rd edn), Basingstoke: Palgrave Macmillan.

Means, R., Richards, S. and Smith, R. (2008) *Community Care: Policy and Practice* (4th edn), Basingstoke: Palgrave Macmillan.

Means, R. and Smith, R. (1985) *The Development of Welfare Services for Elderly People*, London: Croom Helm.

Means, R. and Smith, R. (1998) *From Poor Law to Community Care: The Development of Welfare Services for Elderly People, 1939–1971*, Bristol: Policy Press.

Mental Health Foundation (2010) *Older People*, London: Mental Health Foundation, available at http://www.mentalhealth.org.uk/help-information/mental-health-a-z/O/older-people/ (accessed 16 September 2011).

Milner, J. and O'Byrne, P. (2009) *Assessment in Social Work* (2nd edn), Basingstoke: Palgrave.

Morris, G. and Morris, J. (2010) *The Dementia Care Workbook,* Buckingham: Open University Press.

Munro, E. (2011) *The Munro Review of Child Protection, Interim Report: The Child's Journey*, London: Department of Education.

Murphy, J., Tester, S., Hubbard, G., Downs, M. and MacDonald, C. (2005) Engabling frail older people with a communication difficulty to

References **189**

express their views: The use of Talking Mats™ as an interview tool, *Health and Social Care in the Community* 13(2): 95–107.

National Audit Office (2005) *Reducing Brain Damage: Faster Access to Stroke Care*, London: NAO.

National End of Life Care Programme (2010) *Supporting People to Live and Die Well*, Leicester: National End of Life Care Programme, available at http://www.endoflifecareforadults.nhs.uk/ (accessed 16 September 2011).

Nelson, F. (2006) Nation still divided by poverty and inequality, *The Scotsman*, 4 January, http://news.scotsman.com/scotland/A-nation-still-divided-by.2739234.jp (accessed 16 September 2011).

Newbigging, K. and Lowe, J. (2005) *Direct Payments and Mental Health: New Directions*, York: Joseph Rowntree Foundation.

Nolan, M., Grant, G. and Keady, J. (1998) *Assessing the Needs of Family Carers: A Guide for Practitioners*, Brighton: Pavilion.

Nyman, S. R., Gosney, M. A. and Victor, C. (2010) The psychosocial impact of vision loss on older people, *Generations Review*, April, available at http://www.britishgerontology.org/DB/gr-editions-2/generations-review/the-psychosocial-impact-of-vision-loss-on-older-pe.html (accessed 16 September 2011).

O'Keefe, M., Hills, A., Doyle, M. *et al.* (2007) *UK Study of the Abuse and Neglect of Older People: Prevalence Survey Report*, London: Comic Relief and Department of Health.

Office for National Statistics (2007) *Marriage and Divorce Statistics, 2007*, Newport: ONS, available at http://www.statistics.gov.uk/hub/population/families/marriages—cohabitations—civil-partnerships-and-divorces (accessed 16 September 2011).

Office for National Statistics (2009) *Life Expectancy at Birth*, Newport: ONS, available at http://www.statistics.gov.uk/hub/population/deaths/life-expectancies (accessed 16 September 2011).

Office for National Statistics (2010a) *Focus on Older People: Older People's Day*, Newport: ONS, available at http://www.statistics.gov.uk/hub/population/ageing/older-people (accessed 16 September 2011).

Office for National Statistics (2010b) *Number of Centenarians Grow*, Newport: ONS, available at http://www.statistics.gov.uk/hub/population/ageing/older-people (accessed 16 September 2011).

Oliver, M. and Sapey, B. (2006) *Social Work with Disabled People*, Basingstoke: BASW/Palgrave Macmillan.

Øvretveit, J. (1997) How to describe interprofessional working, in J. Øvretveit, P. Mathias and T. Thompson (eds) *Interprofessional Working for Health and Social Care*, Basingstoke: Macmillan, pp 9–33.

Pannell, J., Means, R. and Morbey, H. (2002) *Surviving at the Margins*, London: Help the Aged/Hact/Crisis.

Parker, H., McArthur, M. and Poxton, R. (2007) *Adult Social Care in Prisons: A Strategic Framework*, Birmingham: University of Birmingham/Care Services Improvement Partnership West Midlands.

Parker, J. and Bradley, G. (2010) *Social Work Practice, Assessment, Planning, Intervention and Review*, Exeter: Learning Matters.

Parliamentary and Health Service Ombudsman (2011) *Care and Compassion? Report of the Health Service Ombudsman on Ten Investigations into NHS Care of Older People*, London: Parliamentary and Health Service Ombudsman, available at http://www.ombudsman.org.uk/__data/assets/pdf_file/0016/7216/Care-and-Compassion-PHSO-0114web.pdf (accessed 5 June 2011).

Parry, G. (1990) *Coping with Crisis*, London: Routledge.

Payne, M. (2002) Coordination and teamwork, in R. Adams, L. Dominelli and M. Payne (eds) *Critical Practice in Social Work*, Basingstoke: Palgrave, pp. 252–61.

Payne, M. (2005) *Modern Social Work Theory*, Basingstoke: Palgrave Macmillan.

Perrin, T. and May, H. (2000) *Wellbeing in Dementia: An Occupational Approach for Therapists and Carers*, London: Harcourt.

Petersen, T. (2004) The developing world: A short window to address global ageing problems, Guest editorial, *Generations Review*, 14(1): 2–4.

Phillips, J. (1992) *Private Residential Care: The Admission Process and Reactions of the Public Sector*, Aldershot: Avebury.

Phillips, J., Bernard, M., Phillipson, C. and Ogg, J. (2002) Social Support in later life: A study of three areas, *British Journal of Social Work* 30(6): 837–54.

Phillips, J., Ray, M. and Ogg, J. (2003) Ambivalence and confict in ageing families: European perspectives, *Retraite en Societe* 38: 80–108.

Phillipson, C. (2002) The frailty of old age, in M. Davies (ed.) *The Blackwell Companion to Social Work*, Oxford: Blackwell, pp. 58–63.

Phillipson, C., Bernard, M., Phillips, J. and Ogg, J. (2001) *The Family and Community Life of Older People: Social Networks and Social Support in Three Urban Areas*, London: Routledge.

Pickard, L., Wittenberg, R., Comas-Herrera, A., Darton, R. and Davies, B. (2000) Relying on informal care in the new century? Informal care for elderly people in England to 2031, *Ageing and Society* 20(6): 745–72.

Pillemar, K. and Luscher, K. (eds) (2004) *Intergenerational Ambivalences: New Perspectives on Parent–Child Relations in Later Life*, New York: Elsevier.

Policy Research Institute on Ageing and Ethnicity (2005) *Black and Minority Ethnic Elders in the UK: Health and Social Care Research Findings*, Leeds: PRIAE.

Post, S. (2000) The concept of Alzheimer's Disease in a hypercognitive society, in K. Maurer and J. F. Ballenger (eds) *Concepts of Alzheimer's Disease: Biological, Clinical and Cultural Perspectives*, Baltimore, MD: Johns Hopkins University Press, pp. 245–56.

Postle, K. (2001) The social work side is disappearing. I guess it started with us being called Care Managers, *Practice* 13 (1): 13–25.

Price, E. (2008) Pride or prejudice? Gay men, lesbians and dementia, *British Journal of Social Work* 38: 1337–52.

Priestley, M. (2004) *Disability: A Life Course Approach,* Basingstoke: Palgrave Macmillan.

Pritchard, J. (1997) Vulnerable people taking risks: Older people and residential care. in H. Kemshall and J. Pritchard (eds) *Good Practice in Risk Assessment and Risk Management (2): Protection, Rights and Responsibilities,* London: Jessica Kingsley.

Pritchard, J. and Leslie, S. (2011) *Recording Skills in Safeguarding Adults: Best Practice and Evidential Requirements,* London: Jessica Kingsley.

Rapoport, L. (1970) Crisis intervention as a mode of brief treatment, in R. Roberts and R. Nee (eds) *Theories of Social Casework,* Chicago: University of Chicago Press.

Ray, M. (2006) Informal care in the context of long-term marriage: The challenge to practice, *Practice* 18: 129–42.

Ray, M., Bernard, M. and Phillips, J. (2009) *Critical Issues in Social Work with Older People,* Basingstoke: Palgrave Macmillan.

Recoop (2010) *Recoop's Vision,* Bournemouth: Recoop, available at http://www.recoop.org.uk/pages/home/ (accessed 16 September 2011).

Rees, P. and Manthorpe, J. (2010) Managers' and staff experiences of adult protection allegations in mental health and learning disability residential services: A qualitative study, *British Journal of Social Work* 40(2): 513–29.

Reid, W. and Epstein, L. (1972) *Task-Centred Casework,* New York: Columbia University Press.

Reid, W. and Shyne, A. (1969) *Brief and Extended Casework,* New York: Columbia University Press.

Renshaw, C. (2008) Do self-assessment and self-directed support undermine traditional social work with disabled people? *Disability and Society* 23(3): 283–6.

Richards, S. (2000) Bridging the divide: Elders and the assessment process, *British Journal of Social Work* 30(1): 37–49.

Rowlands, O. and Parker, G. (1998) *Informal Carers. An Independent Study Carried Out by the Office for National Statistics on Behalf of the Department of Health as Part of the 1995 General Household Survey,* London: HMSO.

Royal College of Psychiatry (2008) Depression and Older Adults, London: Royal College of Psychiatry, available at http://www.rcpsych.ac.uk/ mentalhealthinfoforall/problems/depression/depressioninolderadults. aspx (accessed 16 September 2011).

Royal College of Psychiatry (2010) *National Audit of Dementia (Care in General Hospitals), Interim Report,* London: Royal College of Psychiatry, available at http://www.rcpsych.ac.uk/pdf/The%20Interim %20Report.pdf (accessed 16 September 2011).

Royal National Institute of Blind People (2009) *Common Feelings about Sight Loss,* London: RNIB, available at http://www.rnib.org.uk/livingwithsightloss/copingwithsightloss/emotionalsupport/Pages/common_feelings.aspx (accessed 16 September 2011).

Saleeby, D. (2008) *The Strengths Perspective in Social Work* (5th edn), Harlow: Pearson.

Scharf, T. and Bartlam, B. (2006) *Rural Disadvantage: Quality of Life and Disadvantage amongst Older People – A Pilot Study,* London: Commission for Rural Communities.

Scharf, T., Phillipson C., Smith A. and Kingston, P. (2002) *Growing Older in Socially Deprived Areas,* London: Help the Aged.

Scharf, T., Phillipson, C. and Smith, A. E. (2005) *Multiple Exclusion and Quality of Life amongst Excluded Older People in Disadvantaged Neighbourhoods,* London: Social Exclusion Unit, Office of the Deputy Prime Minister.

Schiller, N., Basch, L. and Blanc-Szanton, C. (eds) (1992) *Towards a Transnational Perspective on Migration: Race, Class, Ethnicity, and Nationalism Reconsidered,* New York: New York Academy of Sciences.

Scourfield, P. (2007) Helping older people in care homes remain citizens, *British Journal of Social Work* 37: 1135–52.

Scragg, T. and Mantell, A. (2008) (eds) *Safeguarding Adults in Social Work,* Exeter: Learning Matters.

Scrutton, S. (1989) *Counselling Older People: A Creative Response to Ageing,* London: Edward Arnold.

Seden, J. (1999) *Counselling Skills in Social Work Practice,* Buckingham: Open University Press.

Sheldon, B. (1995) *Cognitive-Behavioural Therapy: Research, Practice and Philosophy,* London: Routledge.

Signpost (2011) Want to be a broker? Maidstone: Signpost, http://www.signpostuk.org/personal-budgets-brokerage/want-be-broker (accessed 16 September 2011).

Silverman, E. and Della-Giustina, J.-A. (2001) Urban policy and the fear of crime, *Urban Studies* 38(5–6): 941–57.

Simmons, J., Griffiths, R. and Conlon, R. (2010) *CBT for Beginners,* Los Angeles: Sage.

Smale, G., Tuson, G., Biehal, N. and Marsh, P. (1993) *Empowerment, Care Management and the Skilled Worker,* London: NISW.

Smale, G., Tuson, G. and Statham, D. (2000) *Social Work and Social Problems: Working Towards Social Inclusion and Social Change,* Basingstoke: Palgrave.

Social Care Institute for Excellence (2005) *Helping Older People to Take Prescribed Medication in Their Own Home: SCIE briefing,* London: SCIE, http://www.scie.org.uk/publications/briefings/files/briefing15.pdf (accessed 16 September 2011).

Social Care Institute for Excellence (2010) *At a Glance 29: Personalisation Briefing – Implications for Social Workers in Adults' Services*, London: SCIE, http://www.scie.org.uk/publications/ataglance/ataglance29.asp (accessed 16 September 2011).

Social Work Task Force Reform Board (2010) *Building a Safe and Confident Future: One Year On*, London: Department of Education.

Stevenson, O. (2001) Old people at risk, in P. Parsloe (ed.) *Risk Assessment in Social Care and Social Work*, London: Jessica Kingsley, pp. 201–16.

Stroebe, M. S. and Schut, H. (1999) The dual process model of coping with bereavement: Rationale and descripton, *Death Studies* 23: 197–224.

Stroebe, M. S. and Shut, H. (2001) Models of coping with bereavement: A review, in M.S. Stroebe, R.O. Hansson, W. Stroebe and H. Schut (eds) *Handbook of Bereavement Research: Consequences, Coping and Care*, Washington, DC: American Psychological Association, pp. 375–405.

Stroke Association (2010) *About Stroke*, London: Stroke Association, available at http://www.stroke.org.uk/information/about_stroke/index.html (accessed 16 September 2011).

Tanner, D. (2010) *Managing the Ageing Experience: Learning from Older People*, Bristol: Policy Press.

Taylor, B. J. and Donnelly, M. (2006) Professional perspectives on decision-making about the long-term care of older people, *British Journal of Social Work* 36(5): 807–26.

Thompson, N. (1995) *Age and Dignity: Working with Older People*, Aldershot: Arena.

Thompson, N. (2002) *People Skills* (2nd edn), Basingstoke: Palgrave Macmillan.

Thompson, N. (2003) *Communication and Language: A Handbook of Theory and Practice*, Basingstoke: Palgrave.

Thompson, N. (2006) *Anti-Discriminatory Practice* (3rd edn). Basingstoke: Palgrave.

Thompson, N. (2009) *Understanding Social Work*, Basingstoke: Palgrave Macmillan.

Tibbs, M. A. (2001) *Social Work and Dementia: Good Practice and Care Management*, London: Jessica Kingsley.

Titterton, M. (2001) Training professionals in risk assessment and risk management: What does the research tell us?, in P. Parsloe (ed.) *Risk Assessment in Social Care and Social Work: Research Highlights in Social Work*, 36. London: Jessica Kingsley, pp. 217–48.

Tobin, S. (1996) A non-normative old age contrast: Elderly parents caring for offspring with mental retardation, in V. Bengtson (ed.) *Adulthood and Ageing: Research on Continuities and Discontinuities*, New York: Springer.

Tomassini, C. (2005) *Focus on Older People: Demographic Profile*, London: Office for National Statistics.

Trevithick, P. (2005) *Social Work Skills: A Practice Handbook*, Buckingham: Open University Press.

Truak, C. B. and Carkhuff, R. R. (1967) *Towards Effective Counselling and Psychotherapy*, Chicago: Aldine.

Twigg, J. and Atkin, K. (1994) *Carers Perceived: Policy and Practice in Informal Care*, Buckingham: Open University Press.

Vallelly, S., Evans, S., Fear, T. and Means, R. (2006) *Opening Doors to Independence: Older People with Dementia and Extra Care Sheltered Housing*, Bristol: Housing 21.

Victor, C., Scambler, S. J. Bowling, A. and Bond, J. (2005) The prevalence of, and risk factors for, loneliness in later life: A survey of older people in Great Britain, *Ageing and Society* 25: 357–75.

Vincent, J. (2003) *Old Age*, London: Routledge.

Waine, B. and Henderson, J. (2003) Managers, managing and managerialism, in J. Henderson and D. Atkinson (eds) *Managing Care in Context*, London: Routledge/Open University, pp. 49–74.

Waters, J. and Neale, R. (2010) Older people's perceptions of personal safety in deprived communities: understanding the social causes of fear of crime, *Quality in Ageing and Older Adults* 11(1): 48–56.

Wenger, C. (1984) *The Supportive Network*, London: George Allen and Unwin.

Westerhof, G. J. and Tulle, E. (2007) Meanings of ageing and old age: Discursive contexts, social attitudes and personal identities, in J. Bond, S. Peace, F. Dittman-Kohli and G. Westerhof, *Ageing in Society* (3rd edn), London: Sage, pp. 235–54.

Wilcock, K. (2006) *The Meaning of Activity for Older Homeless People*, London: Help the Aged.

World Health Organisation (2010) *Age-friendly Environments Programme*, Geneva: WHO, available at http://www.who.int/ageing/age_friendly_cities/en/index.html (accessed 16 September 2011).

Yost, E., Beutler, L., Corbishley, M. and Allender, J. (1987) *Group Cognitive Therapy: A Treatment Approach for Depressed Older Adults*, New York: Pergamon.

Index